How Not Totally Put Your Children off God

A conversation on Christian parenting
between a father and his sons

HOWARD WORSLEY

MONARCH
BOOKS

For my students at Trinity College, Bristol,
who mirror my efforts in "parenting for faith",
ask for tips as to how this is done and
teach me new ideas from their wisdom

Published by
Lion Hudson Limited
Wilkinson House, Jordan Hill Business Park
Banbury Road, Oxford OX2 8DR, England
www.lionhudson.com

ISBN 978 0 85721 957 2
eISBN 978 0 85721 958 9

First edition 2020

Acknowledgments
Thanks to Howard's sons Nathanael, Jonathan, and Benjamin Worsley for their
contributions to the book.

Scripture quotations marked NIV taken from the Holy Bible, New International
Version Anglicized. Copyright © 1979, 1984, 2011 Biblica, formerly International Bible
Society. Used by permission of Hodder & Stoughton Ltd, an Hachette UK company.
All rights reserved. "NIV" is a registered trademark of Biblica. UK trademark number
1448790.
Scripture quotations marked KJV taken from the Holy Bible, The Authorized (King
James) Version. Rights in the Authorized Version are vested in the Crown. Reproduced
by permission of the Crown's patentee, Cambridge University Press.
Scriptures quotations marked GNB are from the Good News Bible © 1994 published
by the Bible Societies/HarperCollins Publishers Ltd UK, Good News Bible © American
Bible Society 1966, 1971, 1976, 1992. Used with permission.

A catalogue record for this book is available from the British Library

Printed and bound in the UK, March 2020, LH26

"Howard Worsley says it 'as it is' for all who would truly risk parenting for faith. He acknowledges immense joy and abject failure while investing hands-on in story, adventure, and prayer alongside his three boys. Eloquently and impressively, their voices of experience tell it 'as it was' for them. This is a dangerous book full of possibility, reality, and reflection for those who desire to let God be the parent of their children. Don't just read it – practice it, if you dare!"
The Rt Revd Peter Hill, Bishop of Barking

"How Not to Totally Put Your Children Totally Off God *is more than a book, it is a pearl of great price written by a master storyteller. Howard writes with honesty, vulnerability, imagination and humour. Each chapter is a wellspring of wisdom, insight, and theological reflection that reveals the love of a father for his sons and his God. The contributions of Howard's sons beautifully root the unfolding narrative in the reality of their family life and ongoing journey of faith, enriching the text and the experience of the reader. This is such a timely book for all parents – and especially fathers – who long to encourage their children and grandchildren to follow the ancient way of faith."*
Revd Canon Jonathan Triffitt, Rector at Blandford Forum and Langton Long

"*Fantastically funny, utterly compelling and honest, Worsley and sons depict what it means for us not to pass on adult faith to children, but to join with God in helping them discover faith for themselves. This book is brilliant for parents but could easily be applied to anyone who works with children and young people.*"
Revd Thea Smith, Curate at Christ Church Woking

Contents

Foreword

by Ruth Worsley, Bishop of Taunton

I remember one Sunday morning not so long ago, when "bishoping" around our diocese, I had a number of conversations with churchwardens and other committed churchgoers about their children. They were mourning the fact that their children no longer went to church. Had they put them off by offering them a choice? Or was it because their children felt forced into participation? I'm afraid I didn't have a formula to offer.

This book tells a personal story of our family. With two clergy parents, our boys had little choice about going to church. Serving in two different parishes meant that we had no partner to look after the children while we did the God stuff, so we often found ourselves roping the children in to help in readings, prayers, and preparation. It wasn't long before they wanted a greater say!

Our boys haven't always found church a comfortable place to be. Now young adults, their faith in God remains; in the church it is shakier. They've stuck with it, however, despite one being told that the Lent groups at his local church were full… he's started his own "pub theology". One has found that his somewhat wild appearance means he's often mistaken for someone who needs ministering to rather than having profound thoughts himself. And the other is now exploring whether he should become a vicar.

Research tells us that many people find faith in their early, formative years. However, many of them then fall out of churchgoing habits. Some may rediscover that practice later, when they have their own children or when crisis hits. This book isn't just about the discipleship habits such as churchgoing that many parents grew up with; it points to those that may help children to discover something of the vastness and wonder of God.

"Growing Faith" is the most recent initiative from the Church of England's education team that is challenging the church to think about how it can help children, young people, and their families to grow in Christian faith. The valuable thing about "Growing Faith" is that the focus is not just on how the church can attract children and young people to join, or how our church schools can develop a stronger Christian ethos. These have both been and remain important strategies in living, telling, and sharing the story of God's love. However, "Growing Faith" goes a step further in recognizing that there is a growing vacuum in "household" faith, in the passing-on of faith through home relationships. Perhaps families have relied too heavily in the past on the church or school to do the parenting of faith for them.

But this is a two-way process. It isn't just about how we parent our children into faith, but how they challenge, deepen and nurture our faith too. I've often remembered my eighteen-month-old placing his hand on my tummy when I was experiencing birth pangs and saying, "Mummy pray." It led to me taking the simple faith of a child more seriously and including the children in our church to pray alongside their family in healing ministry at all-age worship.

Many of the practices Howard refers to in this book result from his own Franciscan Rule of Life. Taking time to read to the boys was a central part of that Rule. There were times when observance of the Rule went too far, in my opinion. Waking up the children when I'd just got them to bed, to hear their dad read the nightly story down the phone when he was away, didn't make a lot of sense to me, their mum, who had to get them up the next day! However, when they come home now and we share Compline together, I can see the legacy it has left.

Howard's words ring true: "As parents we must learn how to speak our own deepest convictions with poetry and with ritual to allow our children to catch their echoes and to taste their flavour. Then our children will be able to enter our story and make their own choices."

Introduction

This book has grown out of a slow conviction that it had to be written.

I like to think that I'm a regular guy who happens to be ordained. I'm passionate about rugby, camping on remote hillsides in mid-winter, riding motorbikes, reading theology, and being a priest. In the midst of all this, probably the most important thing that happened to me was becoming a dad, and being a dad has been my greatest passion of all.

I always felt that it was tough to be brought up in a vicarage, because so many people seem to think that vicars' kids must be well balanced and privileged, and therefore ought to be perfect. In reality they are normal children who are living their lives on display, as if they were goldfish in a bowl. So it became of special interest to me that my children were OK about their lot in life. Like all parents, I want the best for my children (I really ought to say "we", because these children are a joint effort, but it's me who is writing and I want to take ownership in offering my perspectives). As a parent I've always wanted my boys (we have three) to grow up happy, well educated and able to get on with others, but there is another thing I've desired: that they would find their own faith in God. This has been a deep hope that I have not always articulated, in case it sounded as though I wanted to brainwash my children with my own world views, but actually it is part of my desire that they would find the treasure I have discovered in having a personal faith. If I'm honest, I was also keen that my boys would be able to cope with church, despite all the problems attached to corporate religious movements. It was because of this that I researched a PhD in the 1990s, on how faith discovered in childhood would be a resource across an adult's life.

So when Lion Hudson approached me, I thought they were interested in my wider academic writing on how children discern God. It soon became clear that my academic voice was less interesting to them than my experiential voice, my inner call to say it "as it is" without footnote and without evidencing every single point. I was told that parents are more likely to listen to the voice of other parents than to "pontificating academics" and that the book must be of practical use rather than theoretical interest.

Developing this style has taken a lot of patience, because I feel less safe in offering raw experience about something as complex as parenting. Having written for most of my life for people who are studying for university degrees, I have needed to learn a different way of writing – one that values raw insight more than academic theory.

I have felt anxious that by writing about parenting I might be putting forward the idea that I am perfect as a parent, that my bumbling efforts are actually better than they are. So I have merged my deep convictions of parenting with examples of both "When it worked" and "When it did not work". I have also elicited the help of my sons to write their perspectives on how their experiences and memories connect with (or differ from) my own.

For the record, at the time of writing I am fifty-seven years old and I am passionate about parenting and want to share what I have discovered so far. I have been married to Ruth for thirty-five years. We have three sons, who are now aged thirty-one, twenty-nine, and twenty-six. The older two are married and the youngest is engaged to be married. All three lads have a working Christian faith that is distinctly different from my own and from one another's. Our oldest son Nathanael recently worked as a senior instructor at a Christian outdoors centre in Scotland where among his more evangelical colleagues he was seen as the "liberal theologian". He is not content with simplistic answers about God or faithful action. I was intrigued to hear about his recent call to minister in the church. Our middle son Jonathan works as a teacher for challenging young people in Scotland and is trying to make time to write poetry and drama, having just got married. Before getting married, he spent time living in a Franciscan friary and travelling. His conviction is that God is less known than we think, so he is always looking for space to see mystery. Our youngest son Ben is a teacher in London and is bemused by the awkwardness shown by churches attempting to welcome young people (like him). He is learning to fit into a local church that he values because it is involved in social action, even though he initially felt he did not belong there.

I was ordained in 1993 when Nathanael was six years old, Jonathan was four, and Ben was one. Two years later Ruth was also ordained. She is now a bishop and I am a theological tutor teaching missiology at Trinity College in Bristol.

Parenting for faith

Parenting can be the best or worst of times. It can be a role we love best or one that causes great insecurity. There is no formal training for parenthood. There are no clear benchmarks of success, and yet it demands all our resources, skills, and attention. Parenting has no blueprint. The natural world offers us many examples of sacrificial giving by animal parents and we realize that this self-giving task is not unique to higher-level human intelligence.

But how about parenting for faith? Can we make a difference? Can this be achieved in our rapidly changing twenty-first century? Or is it beyond our control?

Christian parents certainly do not know the ultimate secret of successful parenting any more than other subgroups of parents. While the Bible is littered with good and bad examples of parenting, it is not a manual that tells us how to pass on our faith successfully. Still, every Christian parent wants to communicate their faith to the next generation, to fulfil an ancient command articulated 3,000 years ago by the psalmist of Israel who wrote:

> We will not hide [the teaching of the Lord] from their
> descendants;
> we will tell the next generation
> the praiseworthy deeds of the Lord,
> his power, and the wonders he has done.
> He decreed statutes for Jacob
> and established the law in Israel,
> which he commanded our ancestors
> to teach their children,

so that the next generation would know them,
even the children yet to be born,
and they in turn would tell their children.
Then they would put their trust in God.

(Psalm 78:4–7)

These powerful words awaken a hope in parents who want to pass on their faith in God. Here the psalmist is suggesting that parents are only one part of a chain of faith that started long before they ever existed and which will continue many generations after them. It is the village that brings up the child, or maybe the wider family context: those who went before and those coming after.

Many parents think they are doing a poor job simply because they have never been told that the love they show their children is amazing. Surrounded by the complexities of their growing children and their own inner uncertainties, they are often dismayed by their own levels of intolerance with their children. They kick themselves because they cannot get their children to be approximately compliant, let alone well behaved. In the world of the church, many Christian parents feel desperately concerned that their children no longer own the faith expressed when they were smaller and are worried that they have not nurtured the fragile seed of faith. What did they do wrong in passing on the story of faith?

This book is particularly for those people. It is a book of hope and heroic failure that has at its heart the theological idea that it is God who is the ultimate parent and it is God who parents within each one of us.

I would argue that it shouldn't really be the parents' problem if faith is not passed on to the next generation. If the parental belief is to pass the parental understanding of faith on to their children, then isn't that more about parental ego? It is not their responsibility. (BW)

(This comment is offered by Ben Worsley (BW), and he is the first of our three sons to give an alternative or similar viewpoint to mine in the text. The three boys are introduced below, and their various contributions appear throughout.)

The message of this book is that parents are partners with God. Our task is to look after God's children, so we must learn to share that responsibility with God. Christian parenting is best achieved when we have discovered a vision of kingdom parenting (doing it God's way) and then learned how to build kingdom habits so that our families live with Christian habits that are naturally engrained.

The book

Each chapter has two sections. Section A contains reflections on habits that seemed to work for me in passing on my faith to my sons. Section B then reflects on the same habits but from a more critical perspective. These five chapters come from my experiences as a dad, a Christian leader, and a theologian. They can be seen as those habits that I believe in passionately. They are the "Dos" – those habits that I have formed in parenting for faith. They emerged in the business of parenting and have become clearer to me as I look back and reflect on the journey so far. They are the essential forces that have helped me on the great adventure of bringing up children with a Christian world view. They describe those times when being a parent felt as though life was slotting into place.

The "Dos" are:

- telling stories;
- going on adventures and making memories;
- praying;
- philosophizing;
- going to church (as part of the kingdom dream).

We sewed these habits into our lives in the form of regular rituals as we began to raise our children. All of them tended to fall into my domain as father. If my wife Ruth were writing this book, I think she would identify different habits.

- *Storytelling:* the most foundational part of the day. We would lock out the day and read a book together. It was linked to praying and to philosophizing as part of the end of the day.
- *Going on adventures:* we planned and looked forward to these, and they were linked to "making memories", seizing the day, doing something we would not forget by building for the future.
- *Praying:* the crucial means of letting God speak to us at key moments, when we were more consciously aware of him filtering through the very warp and woof of our lives.
- *Philosophizing:* reflecting on the day that was ending.
- *Going to church:* the final habit of going to church and meeting people who were not the same as us.

Section B of each chapter contains the nightmares that skulk around the edges of consciousness – the failures, where I set out with high hopes that were not realized. However, it could have been in these "cock-ups" that the actual parenting for faith was really carried out. These negative habits were:

- *Fluffing my lines:* when the truth claims of the Bible stories appeared implausible compared to the actions of the day. Or when the made-up story we were reading together appeared to have far more power than the Scriptures.
- *Irresponsible adventures:* when good plans ended up in virtual chaos. We didn't create good memories, and God seemed a long way away, and talking about him made no sense.
- *The "dark night of the soul":* when we could not talk about God through prayer, since we were not sure that he was there.
- *Being vacuous:* when we sensed we were not being honest as we philosophized about life or God, and when we could not admit that we were simply spinning threads instead of ropes.
- *Despising church:* when church appeared to be a place of hypocrisy and boredom that could cause a strange paralysis.

Introduction to the writers

Nathanael Worsley (NW)

Nathanael is the oldest son (thirty-one). He is the qualified outdoor instructor who does the outdoors properly and is now setting off with his wife on a long journey in a van.

I have found trying to help Dad by adding to this book very difficult. Call on me any time for a robust discussion about religion and faith, where I am at liberty to put out an opinion and then later withdraw it, or even to lay out conflicting thought processes simultaneously as I work out where my stance lies. The liquid ebb and flow of talking is where I am comfortable. But ask me to chain down my thoughts with ink and paper and you have me running scared. Nevertheless, I have done my best not to waffle in trying to tell you that this is what I mean while it is nothing of the kind! No wonder the biggest insult my family could lay at my door is to call me a diplomat or politician. I hope that what I write is clear . . . that my yes is yes and my no is no. I have given a brief sense of my reactions and perceptions to Dad's five reflections alongside my own thoughts. (NW)

Jonathan Worsley (JW)

Jonathan is the middle son (twenty-nine). He has longish hair and blackish clothes – a bit like a knight, a bit like a hobo. He is also a poet, a traveller to forgotten places.

What sort of image does the word "parent" conjure? It is an impersonal, broad, and bland word, used by schools and official letters to ask mums and dads to give consent or censure, or add their authority. This book should not be about parents, or worse still about parenting, but rather about kin. It is about family and the deep, growing, changeable bond between children and their grown-ups. It will seek to avoid advice and it will reflect the relationships that brought it into being: subjective, chaotic, and human. (JW)

Benjamin Worsley (BW)

Benjamin is the youngest son (twenty-six). He's currently a bit trendier than some, but that could be because he is still single. He teaches in a primary school.

As I note Dad's sections on "what went wrong" (when he parented) I am reminded of the comment "with the help of the thorn in my foot, I spring higher than anyone with sound feet". But actually this seems to suggest that what doesn't kill you makes you stronger. I like the idea that with the help of the thorn, at least I will jump instead of remaining standing still. These "cock-ups" of parenting are clearly at least as important as the good habits. I have enjoyed reading these the most. (BW)

For discussion

Before reading further, stop and ask yourself:

- What are the "Dos" and "Don'ts" that you would offer in the hope of passing on faith to the next generation?
- Where did you get these ideas from? Are they derived from your parents or in reaction to them?
- How do you respond to the idea of having children (grown-up sons) commenting on parental "wisdom"?
- What do you think of Nathanael's comment below?

Before we start, the thing that struck me is that while Dad has clearly separated each chapter into "When it worked" and "When it did not work", this logical separating of good from bad is not how it works in the real world. Things have a habit of growing together and it's not until much later that you can determine whether the fruit is sweet or bitter. This to me draws very strong parallels with Jesus' parable of the wheat and the chaff. This I'll come back to in my comments. (NW)

CHAPTER 1

Telling Stories

(A) When Storytelling Revealed Truth

Then [having reflected on the Scriptures with Jesus] their eyes were opened and they recognised him.
(Luke 24:31)

Storytelling as truth

Parents who want to pass on a true story of faith are guided by a story that is greater than they are. They know they are part of a faith that existed long before their birth and will continue long after they have died. Their faith provides a map by which they make sense of life, directing their pathway and offering a vision for Christian parenting.

In parenting for Christian faith, we believe that our map is the true story of faith. As Christians we believe it is written about in the Bible. It is lived out in the family. It is also what is passed on when no one is looking.

The true story (the accurate map of faith)

True stories are sensed by the heart as well as by the head. They have a ring of truth about them. So when we hear the true story that God created us, that God loves us, and that God forgives us, something deep inside us is challenged to believe it. Foundational to the role of being a parent who passes on faith is acquiring the sense of being loved.

> I feel it worth mentioning (right from the start) that I am sceptical about "truth claims", but I have a reverence for stories. I agree with Schiller that: "Deeper meaning resides in the fairy tales told me in my childhood than any truth that is taught in life.[1]" (JW)

Sensing that we are loved is the true map from which Christian parents plot themselves in order to find their bearings. I can well remember becoming a dad for the first time and feeling unbelievably ill-equipped. How could I, a very child in the experience of life, be expected to be an adequate parent? I found the ancient narratives of the Bible arising to guide me, but it was not any particular biblical story that was of help – it was the overall story. It was the "flavour" of the Bible that came to my rescue rather than any single text. I found that I was drawing on the general themes that run through Scripture. I was gaining energy from the general flow of Scripture, getting drawn into that timeless movement from the very beginnings of history, towards its inevitable end. I began to position myself within that flow of history. I was able to sense that history would achieve

---

1 Schiller, Friedich, *The Piccolomini* (1799)

a good outcome; that love would prevail; that in the end the kingdom of God would be revealed.

As a young parent I began to discover that the Bible was fostering a sense of well-being that I needed. Why was this? It was because the Bible has been treasured over the thousands of years of its existence, and it has been an inspiration to millions of parents before me. It was because the Bible has stood the test of time, having been reflected on and studied, prayed over, debated, and wrestled with. It was because there is considerable realism within the Bible that does not allow for an easy interpretation or a simple answer. And for all these reasons I joined the stream of faith that perceives it to be the Word of God, and considered it to be useful for teaching, for encouraging, and for challenging as I began to parent.

The parent's part in the true story

We all live by the personal stories we tell about ourselves. We also live within the story we consider to be true. We all live within a grand narrative that may or may not be known to others. If we are Christians, then we are fed by the ancient Hebrew Scriptures and by the stories of the early church. Our inner geography might be able to picture the desert of Sinai with the vast Red Sea lapping against its shores. We will be able to imagine Jesus and his disciples striding over the hills above a sparkling Lake Galilee.

We also live with an inner personal narrative as to how we fit into that grand narrative. This is how the ancient biblical stories of the Christian tradition make sense to us in our own life story. When we become a parent, the meaning from these stories is what we draw upon to explain the meaning of life to our children.

Parenting is about telling our best stories to our children in order to allow them to find their own way. If their map is accurate, they can begin to navigate life accurately. We need to let our children know what we have found to be true so that they can find out what is true for themselves. They will identify with their own inner story even as they enter into the true story. As parents we want to give our children what is good for them: stories that will nourish and resource them, stories that will feed their souls. But how are we to speak truth when so much of what is true cannot be fully framed in words and when the deepest things in life are experienced rather than taught? How are our children to identify the true story against the many fictitious stories or virtual tales that circulate?

The answer must surely be that the parent has to learn to become a good storyteller. As parents we must learn how to speak our own deepest convictions with poetry and with ritual to allow our children to catch their echoes and to taste their flavour. Then our children will be able to enter our story and make their own choices.

Our stories are about the whole of life as well as about faith. If our stories are all religious, then our children might well wonder if we have ever encountered the world they experience at school, or on TV, or in friendships elsewhere. Just as we send our children to school in order that they experience wide teaching and learning, so our task with our children is to equip them for life. We parent them as younger people who are physical, mental, and spiritual beings inhabiting the real world.

I think the problem here is the idea of what truth is and its attainability. In my eyes it is something that can only be striven for and not really attained. The idea that you can outline one story as truth and one as not demonstrates this. I have had better (i.e. more in-depth) spiritual conversations with Dad about Jostein Gaarder, Philip Pullman, and John Wyndham than about the Bible. (BW)

Therefore our stories must be about the everyday. They must be about real life and the imagined life that is yet to be experienced. Stories will captivate the imagination, connecting with what is already known and what is coming into being.

When it comes to passing on faith to our children, we must do so by telling the story of God in colourful and imaginative ways, not in ways that repress the inquisitive mind or attempt to control them with dogma. After all, we believe that theology is a combination of God's revelation and human attempts to understand that truth. At best our theology will always be partial and never the complete truth. "We see through a glass, darkly" (1 Corinthians 13:12, KJV) in the hope that one day we will see clearly. Even as our faith touches what we long for and senses that time when God is known, we have the complication of communicating this to our children using mere words. In reality we sense that we know more than we can tell. Our personal knowledge is often implicit and makes reference to an interior story that is barely communicable.

As parents we therefore need to find the right stories to communicate the Christian faith. Fortunately we have the Bible, that great storybook of richness containing within it many stories that can be passed on to children at the various stages of their lives. As a map, the Bible is an invaluable tool. It comes with the highest authority, but it does need careful handling, especially when used with children. That is where a parent's life experience comes to their aid, because the parent is the mediator of the story (as the storyteller) and the parent learns to position themselves into the story as they tell it, and then invite their child into the story.

The child's part in the true story

Children will naturally want to enter into a good story. When they are very young, they are more likely to hear the story with rapturous attention and a more complete acceptance. Observers of the process suggest that while young, children are initially pre-critical. Young children perceive the story as a river in which they are being swept along by the current. They sense that they are in the mid-flow of the river – actually in the story. As they hear the story of David and Goliath, they see the size of the giant opposing them, hear his threats, and feel the ground shuddering as he walks, for they have become little David.

This makes storytelling an exciting and a responsible task. It is exciting because it is rewarding to see the rapt attention given by the child. It is a responsible task because the parent needs to present the story without frightening the child, offering sufficient comfort for the story to be safe. As the child becomes capable of critical engagement and when other perspectives become available to them, the parent needs to allow space for more critical reflection. Why did David's brothers not try to beat up Goliath? Why did David not use Saul's armour? How did David become so good at using a sling? Is it possible for a man to grow to nine feet tall or is this a literary device? As the child grows older, he or she is now no longer in the mid-flow of the river but is observing the flow of the story from the bank of the river.

As an adult looking back on my Christian childhood, I can recall mixing up my biblical geography with the landscape outside my window while visiting my grandparents in Scotland, so I wrote a poem entitled "Geography of Childhood". This poem merged biblical geography with the actual geography of Edinburgh. It described the rather severe Christians at the gospel hall attended by my grandparents. In those days, I was in the mid-flow of the river, not able to perceive the difference between what was actual and what was fantasy.

Geography of Childhood

The land before time is laid out
Differently to the maps,
Enclosing unknown places,
Not yet committed to the charts.
The Mount of Olives is the Blackford Hills,
The River Jordan is the Braid Burn and
The distant Pentland Hills beyond Greenbank
Part where the forbidden mountains
Open to the road to Jericho.

The land of the fathers is governed
By the elders,

Bearded and worthy, peering sagely
Over half-moon glasses,
Governing the zone of Truth against the encroaching world,
Guarding the sisters 'gainst the wiles of the evil one,
Their black Bibles sufficient to give evidence,
Their small hymn books
A song of survival.

But their song is strangely quiet now,
Their wrinkled heads
Bowed in dusty grief.
While the child still runs amok in reborn Galilee,
Where the sparkling waters
Gather to hold the sacred feet
And fishes leap at His summons to the net,
And the boy roams
Into the antique land.

This poem carries a sense of the less well-known horizons of the hills around Edinburgh as being the unknown world of the Bible. It depicts a child's vision of the serious adults who attended a Brethren meeting hall and notes that, although they have died out, their faith lives on in the child who once met them. It is a memory of how the story of the Bible merged with the child's story as faith was formed.

The reason why my faith was nurtured effectively at this age was because my grandmother would tell me Bible stories by the fire at night. She told me of Joseph, the boy who grew up to be Prime Minister of Egypt. Then she told me of Samuel, the boy who heard God when the adult priest did not. She also told me of the boy Timothy, who was a third-generation Christian in the early church, and the apostle Paul instructed that no one should look down on his faith. All these were true stories about boys who believed in God. She adapted each one to me and I got the message.

Reading Bible stories with children (the theory)

The key thing in using Scripture with children is that both adult and child are "under" the story. We both sit at God's feet as we discover our story for life. The adult parent is not the mediator between God and the child. When both parent and child encounter the Word of God, they do so as fellow pilgrims. Neither of them possesses the whole truth of God, and neither of them is the sole teacher nor the sole learner. Both sit under God's tutelage.

I will discuss the ways of reading the Bible with children as:

- bad ways (abdication);
- inadequate ways (superficial engagement or unquestioned instruction) and
- good ways (mutual contemplation).

Abdication

There seem to be a lot of bad ways of sharing Bible stories with children, the worst of which is when parents do nothing. This is what happens when parents think their child will encounter the Bible being read in an engaging way at school, at church, in the children's church, or in Sunday school. As a result they do nothing with their children involving the Bible. However, anecdotal research suggests that children are unlikely to have a significant encounter with the Bible unless someone has helped them to do so.

I am glad that the 1960s' trend of suggesting that children should be kept away from the Bible has been largely superseded. This unfortunate practice of perceiving the Bible to be a book that can only be understood by older people was taught by theorists who believed that children's concrete thinking could not understand the abstract language of the Bible. It was suggested that children might be damaged by encountering Bible stories.

This developmental perspective continued to have widespread influence in religious educational circles and in church Sunday schools through the 1970s and 1980s, even though there was a steady critical response from confessional Christian practitioners.

Superficial engagement

The next worst thing is when parents rattle their way through a Bible story out of duty, without reflecting upon it with the child. This method of Bible reading is often superficial and is used by parents who think that it is their duty to familiarize their child with Scripture. However, they might be too sure of the accuracy of their theology or alternatively they might be unsure of their theology. The danger in being too sure is that they use the Bible uncritically, and will teach it literally. This style represses the child's curiosity by not allowing reflection that asks questions.

Similarly, if parents are unsure about their faith, they might opt for a simplistic perspective by teaching all biblical genres as simple fact, implicitly saying that the Bible must be taken at face value without critique. They might try to get the story over as quickly as possible because they are unsure of their own theological thoughts other than that they must help their child to accept the Scriptures as uncritically as they do. By offering no contemplative engagement or critical thought in the process, the parents do not help the children. They could be suppressing critical imagination or reflection.

In this instance, the children are likely to come to the conclusion that the Bible is of high status to the adult but it cannot be questioned, just accepted and believed. Such an attitude by parents might be called "overly reverential", because although it affirms the authority of Scripture, it does so in an unquestioning manner, putting the text ten feet above correction or even beyond reflection. Giving the Bible such a high status that it cannot be debated can lead to a form of disempowerment. In fact, wider research shows that parents who read the Bible to their children without allowing critical reflection tend to cause inertia. By being passive, they abandon their own interpretation in favour of the text's overt meaning. This of course can lead to the children being forced to choose between literalist acceptance of the text and rejection of the faith.

Children who note the tension in this encounter with Scripture might decide that although their parents cannot question the text, maybe they can themselves. They think that even if the Bible seems to say that Balaam's ass talked to him, donkeys cannot talk. They ask themselves how Jesus walked on water. They ask if it is OK to overturn tables in church because you are angry with people.

If children's emergent critical thinking is not allowed to be articulated, it is likely to go underground. Then they may well believe that their parents are not able to offer critical thinking to matters of faith and thereby begin to think that the only option is to not believe in God or the Bible's value.

There seems to be the same rigidity in telling Bible stories both in parents who are unsure of the meaning of the text and in those who have a strong interpretation to pass on. Neither allows for the child's reflection.

Mutual contemplation

By contrast, the best way to read the Bible with children is to tell the story as a disciple who does not know everything. Parents and children are both on the same road of faith. Neither parent nor child is more in command of what the Scripture means today. Both sit under the Word of God as they follow Jesus and both are there to reflect theologically. Obviously the parent will initially be at a higher stage of education, but they do not have all the knowledge of God. When parents tell Bible stories and then open the story up for discussion, they invite their children to become theologians with them. (Why do you think the donkey saw the angel when Balaam didn't? How did Jesus walk on water? Why did Jesus overturn the moneychangers' tables in the Temple?)

When this approach is taken, children are encouraged to reflect on the text as God's Word, and they are also invited to think of its meaning in terms of how they ought to respond to it. When this happens, parents gain the added benefit of learning from their children, of hearing their children's insight. This is often an original fresh vision of reality.

If the parent reads as if they do not know everything it will mean that they have to accept criticism in the form of interpretations with which they are less comfortable. Eternity may be set in the hearts of people, but not all stories are for all times. In other words, the Bible changes as it is heard by different ears – ears which themselves will change as they grow older. (JW)

I have spent a little time researching the phenomenon of what happens when adults become "like little children" and conversely when the child begins to lead. I have written about this in a book called *A Child Sees God* (2013), which records conversations between parents and children after reading the Bible. In this book, I use seven basic genres of story and conclude with six key recommendations as to how to tell Bible stories in ways that are resourceful to parents and children:

1. **Regularity:** storytelling doesn't have to be nightly, but it should at least be weekly.
2. **Importance:** both the teller and the listener should anticipate this event and come prepared.
3. **Timing:** it will be clear when the story will start and also how much time is available for storytelling.
4. **Ambience:** any ritual can be enhanced with extra attention given to lighting, sound, smell, or heat, as well as the use of a particular room or chair.
5. **Sacredness:** storytelling should not be interrupted by the telephone or by another person.
6. **Internal engagement:** all families have their own rules about interruptions from children, but the general

rule is that the story should be told with occasional interruption from the child, otherwise any complex issues of comprehension or discussion will be left until the end, and may be forgotten. Too much interruption could make it difficult to tell the story, however, so some balance is needed.

There is a plethora of children's Bibles on the market, but the key to their value in communicating with children is in the approach that the adult takes in reading as they reflect on the biblical story with the child. Biblical stories are different from the vast array of adventure and fantasy stories available, and as such are not as accessible, but they come with a different value. They are stories for telling at the end of the day before prayers. They are stories to be told over breakfast before school. They are stories to be told in the car on the way somewhere. And, most importantly, they are stories to unlock other stories.

Children might ask how Jesus is similar to (or different from) a super-hero. They might question what it was like when the earth was formed. The parent might wonder with the child as the story is reflected on. For example, "I wonder what heaven will be like," or, "In the story of David and Goliath, I wonder what David felt like as he approached the giant," or, "When Jesus was asleep in the boat in a storm, I wonder what the disciples were thinking."

My earliest memories of my developing faith are completely intertwined with storytelling of all kinds. It wasn't until recently that I realized how unusual this admixture of my faith and my life really was. I have noticed how common, easy, and possibly comfortable it is to keep separate the world of religion and faith from the rest of our "real" lives. This was not the case during my childhood. Most day-to-day events ended up being discussed and viewed through the lens of faith. This was, I think, a direct result of us developing the habit of regularly mixing talk of God, the Bible, faeries, philosophy, adventure, and myth.

The truth is I always felt (and still do) that they all fit together so naturally. Attempting to talk about any one of these subjects is to attempt to talk about things that go beyond human understanding and point toward the divine. (NW)

A helpful means for telling Bible stories to children is found in the work of Jerome Berryman, whose innovative approach to religious education is called "Godly Play". This practical method of engagement encourages adults to become childlike in their work with children. Having outlined his method in his book *Godly Play*, he concludes by saying that godly play is a way to keep open the opportunity for the true self to emerge in childhood and the possibility that adults may return to where they began and begin to grow again.

Berryman writes: "Become like a child if you want to mature as an adult. To play the ultimate game, don't rely on will, belief, denial or reason alone. Play. Play in a Godly way. Play with the Creator" (1995, p. 18). In this way he has made room for the Bible to be used with pre-adolescent children. The Bible can be the truthful map that helps a child to navigate the Christian faith.

Rosemary Cox develops this idea in her work *Using the Bible with Children* by saying, "If we give [children] the skills to explore the Bible for themselves, listen respectfully to their insights and encourage them to find personal applications, then we can begin to discover together" (2000, p. 22).

This process will be resourceful both to the child and to the parent engaging with the child's perception.

Reading (Bible) stories with children (the habit)

However much you try, you cannot make the Bible quite as gripping as an age-appropriate book that has been written specifically for children. A fair amount of editing needs to take place in the telling of the Bible story, as well as the opportunity for pause and reflection.

Personally I can recall finding a children's Bible in the library when I was still at primary school. Before that point I had never picked up the Bible with the intention of reading it. In that school library, I didn't read a single word, but I spent many hours looking at the pictures. One in particular depicted Jesus dying on the cross. As the blood dripped from his wounds, angels were collecting it in bright chalices. I wondered why they were doing this and I remembered that at church on Sunday the blood of Christ was shared around as though it was wine. So I wondered if this was how the blood was gathered to go into the chalice that the adults were drinking from. I wondered when it would run out. I was not sure if I would like to taste the blood when I was older and could take the chalice. When I finally did get to taste it at a Communion service, I was amazed it was so sweet – not like the blood when I cut my finger. I asked for clarification at the Brethren church we attended, but my question caused such shock that I did not pursue it. As a result of this experience, when I became a parent using biblical literature with complex metaphors, I was in two minds as to how I would read the Bible with my boys. Should I tell them that the Holy Communion of bread and wine was not actually Jesus' body and blood, or should I let them work it out for themselves?

I can also recall the profound experience of reading the Bible alone as a ten-year-old. I had met a young woman who had come to our church and she had shown me her own personalized Bible. It had stickers on the front cover and the text was underlined at key points where she had valued what it said. The version of her Bible was more readable than the ones available at the back of our church, so when she lent it to me for a week, I was keen to find out what the book was like. She suggested that I start reading one of the shortest books. She had just read a short book in the Bible called Nahum, so I thought I'd try the next one. It was called Habakkuk. So, one night, as a primary-school-aged child, I started reading one of the minor prophets. It was not a particularly gripping book, but suddenly, halfway through chapter 3, I was overcome by a sense of God's presence. As I read the ancient text, I became aware of the full moon rising in the night sky.

Nearly 3,000 years earlier, Habakkuk had written, "The sun and moon stood still in their habitation: at the light of thine arrows they went, and at the shining of thy glittering spear" (Habakkuk 3:11, KJV). I got out of bed and said my first personal prayers on my knees (this was the first time that I can recall praying for real and on my own). To this day, that memory stands out in my experience with dazzling clarity as being when I took God seriously. When I became a parent, I longed for my sons to have such a theophany moment, but of course, this was not mine to create.

As a boy hearing this story, I wanted to have a profound and magical experience, but it never quite manifested itself in the way I wanted it to. Part of the complexity of growing up with a father who has mythologized hildhood (like a Romantic poet) has been to reconcile imagination and experience, allowing myself to change while fearing what innocent wonder might be lost in changing. However, I still look to see Blake's angels in the trees. (JW)

I have many other memories from my childhood of when the Bible was read, but none have the evocation of these early recollections. Other memories were the regular reading from the Bible that my father did around the breakfast table at 7:30 a.m. He would open a big black Bible and launch into the text. The readings I remembered most were those read from the book of Proverbs, texts directed at young men who were being tempted to run after pretty girls (or so I thought). We never discussed these readings, but the toast often got cold as the reading went on.

Other occasions were the Bible readings at church on a Wednesday evening, which were more reflective but invariably the domain of the more scholarly adults. Much to my dismay, the questions I wanted to ask were not asked, and if I pitched in with a question, it was not given a satisfactory answer. I wanted to know why anything done by people in the Bible was somehow virtuous. Was it OK for David to use a sling to overcome a thug called Goliath when maybe he could have talked him down? Was it OK for Samson to be so violent, or for Solomon to have so many wives? I got the impression that there was a subtext that the adults knew and I did not know, and as an adult looking back, I think I was correct in my assumption.

So what was I to do as a Christian parent if I was to present the Bible to my boys without causing confusion and anxiety?

Initially I told them stories on a walk outside before bed. They loved sitting on my shoulders and I loved carrying them. With our first son on my neck, his little voice inches from my ears, his hands clinging on to my hair or my ears, we would discuss whatever we saw as we walked. Maybe it was the moon climbing high in the sky. Why was it smaller than yesterday? Who made it? How did it shine so brightly? As we walked, I'd tell my son about the moon in the Bible; how God caused the moon to lighten the night sky on the fourth day of creation. I also told him that in the Bible Habakkuk[2] said that one day the moon would stop in its tracks and go no further, because God was coming closer. And I told other stories too: stories about my childhood, stories that I had read when I was younger, or stories that I made up as we walked. All stories were mingled into one mass of imagination, wonder, reflection, and time together. We enjoyed those times – both of us.

When the next child came along, it would be the smallest who was the one privileged to sit on my shoulders, and the other(s) would walk alongside. We would have times for Bible reflection as we walked and times for play. Sometimes we would walk to the local park. This graduated into a bedtime ritual when the boys started school.

---

2 Habakkuk 3:11

School brought a new regime, because tiredness began to creep up on them more. This was when I developed a ritual, because I too was very busy as a parish priest, normally having a meeting every night. We found that the best thing was to gather at a certain time in the sitting room. The time was normally 7 p.m. because evening meetings at church were normally scheduled to start at 7.30. We all had our favourite place. We would turn the gas fire on if it was cold. We would turn on a single lamp, just above my right shoulder, leaving the rest of the room in half-light, and then the story would begin.

The first story to really catch on was *The Lion, the Witch and the Wardrobe* by C. S. Lewis – a story I loved because I could recognize the underlying Christian narrative. This was a book that I had discovered in my own childhood and I had learned to interpret the implicit Christian meanings within it. As I read this to the boys, we only read one chapter at a time, even though we wanted more. After reading came the discussion. After the discussion came the prayers. The schedule became set in stone. It never varied.

Creating the right atmosphere in which to tell stories is something both mystical and pragmatic that continues to fascinate me. When training as a teacher in London, I wrote an essay with the grandiose title "The palace of essential experience", which was all about my attempts to capture something of the magic of our story time while teaching inner-city kids to think analytically (and imaginatively) about literature. I came to the conclusion that ritual is all-important: dimmed lights, comfortable seats on the floor, and a sense of profound reverence for the book in hand. Unfortunately, I found that schools look dimly on the burning of incense, though taking students outside whenever you can escape is something I strongly recommend. (JW)

Actually, proceedings did sometimes vary a bit. One night the diocesan bishop called in "on spec", just as I had started the story. Ruth, my wife, answered the door and told me that the bishop was here. I went to the door, thanked him profusely for visiting, but said I had just started the story and that it was a commitment I needed to fulfil. Would he like to join us or would he like to wait until I'd finished? He decided to join us.

I well remember taking my "boss" into our sacred space. By then we had graduated to lighting a piece of charcoal and burning incense as the story was read. We were halfway through *The Lord of the Rings* by J. R. R. Tolkien and I led the bishop through dense clouds of billowing smoke to find a chair in the half-darkness, then I continued the reading of the chapter. (By the way, in those days most Anglican bishops in our part of the world were rather suspicious of the practice of burning incense, considering it to be a hallmark of the Roman Catholic Church; that is, not Anglican.) The chapter we were reading was the one where Gollum (Smeagol) was debating whether or not to eat the "nice hobbitses". I had perfected a spooky Gollum voice that I felt I had to maintain in the presence of our visitor whom I barely knew. I recall not being particularly embarrassed, although I had ample reason to be so. Fortunately the bishop was a gracious man, and sat patiently and respectfully through the proceedings. After we'd finished the section from Tolkien, we discussed whether Gollum could be saved or whether he was irreparably damaged. This was a very interesting conversation that I still remember, because my eldest son articulated a belief that Gollum would "obviously be saved" and that if God was God "he could do anything", certainly at least save a poor lost Gollum, who had had such a difficult life.

In this conversation I recognized that the theological notion whereby all are saved was a universalist idea and I remained educationally neutral, asking the boys in human terms if everyone would be saved or if anyone would lose out on eternal life. I was met with an unambiguous certainty that all would be saved. My sons, in their early primary school years, were quite clear that Christ Jesus would save the whole world. I recall my thoughts at that time were slightly more anxious as to what the bishop might be thinking in terms of theological accuracy.

Looking back now, as a theological educator, I see that the question we were asking was one of the most complex and sophisticated anyone can ask. After some robust theological discussion between a nine-year-old, a seven-year-old, and a three-year-old, with the bishop listening in, we came to our prayers. All three little voices and mine and the bishop's joined in saying the evening collect that night.

> I loved listening to these stories. I think the ritual was so important. The style, the gravitas, the ceremony. Who would light the incense or who would get the best chair was important. It was certainly a calming environment, as I would fall asleep pretty much every time and be royally offended at missing part of whatever story we were reading. (BW)

Years later, my sons separately told me that the time when the bishop visited was the occasion when they realized how important the story was to me (as well as to them) – so important that even my "boss" did not get to ruin it. They were very pleased that he'd been told he could not interrupt our story.

Another variation was when I had to be away on a conference or leading a retreat. On these occasions I would book in a phone call in the evening at a pre-arranged time and read the story down the phone, and we'd say our prayers over the phone.

Over the years we read all the C. S. Lewis stories, all the Tolkien stories, then all the Philip Pullman series. We were never short of candidates for the next story. Sometimes we "went to the dark side" and began books we thought we'd like but did not, so we learned how to give up occasionally and select a new book. Looking back, I recall that we particularly enjoyed *The Pilgrim's Progress* by John Bunyan, *To Kill a Mockingbird* by Harper Lee, *Life of Pi* by Yann Martel and *The Rogues of Alwyn* by Frank Crisp.

> Some books fall flat when read aloud in this way. Others surprise you. My recommendation is to quit while you're still ahead if a book is sending you to sleep. I agree with Wilde: there are no good or bad books,[3] but they must function first as entertainment. One I particularly remember Dad reading to us was *The Old Man and the Sea*; Hemingway didn't put a word out of place. (JW)

Several times I tried to introduce the Bible as a homily to cap the story, but it never took off as a habit, although the Bible was often discussed as a means of interpreting the story we had been reading.

As the boys grew older, the stories changed. We even read philosophical books like Nietzsche's *Ecce Homo*, but

---

3 Preface to *The Picture of Dorian Gray*: "There is no such thing as a moral or an immoral book. Books are well written, or badly written. That is all."

the practice never stopped as the boys went through their A-Level years. Obviously the break from home when the university years came meant that the story began to be told to only two boys instead of three and then only to one, but the tradition continued.

In some ways it still continues, because when all the boys are back home, we often, for old times' sake, have a story time – normally a short story that one of them wants to share. It is still me who reads it. This year when we went up to Scotland to meet the family of my son's wife-to-be, the subject of storytelling came up and I found myself reading a new story round a fire in the woods one night. The whole family gathered. They wanted to be part of our tradition. It is just as well I am not easily embarrassed.

It was odd that when one by one the other two went off to university, I as a seventeen-year-old boy was still being read stories by Dad, and yet no shame was there. Stories have been told in communities for years. The best chair by the fire was reserved for the storyteller. Unfortunately this is no longer the norm as I am no longer living at home. (BW)

For discussion

- What do you consider to be good ways of reading the Bible with children?
- How can this be done badly?
- How do you position yourself on the map of faith and how does this influence your role in telling the story of faith?
- What is it in the Christian story that you really want to pass on as truth?

For reflection

In Imitation of Larkin

Children also muck you up.
They, accidentally carrying your blood,
May not mean it, but they do,
They will, they will be doing so when you're gone.
They will muck up, they will be screwed by you
And the whole strange circle will roll on.
For love, for love will kill you
Else you'll die knowing it did not.
And which is worse:
To feel the pain
Or never play and never feel the loss? (JW)

(B) When Storytelling Became Myth (Fluffing your lines)

> *Then the devil took [Jesus] to the holy city... "If you*
> *are the Son of God," he said, "throw yourself down, for*
> *it is written: 'He will command his angels concerning*
> *you..." Jesus answered him: "It is also written, 'Do not*
> *put the Lord your God to the test.'"*
>
> **(Matthew 4:5–7)**

In the same way that the true story can lead to correct living, the false story can lead to wasted lives. A parent can be like a ship's navigator who plots the course for their child but finds themselves lost and at sea. This happens when parents' stories prove to be inadequate. They do not say enough. They do not seem plausible. They appear irrelevant or maybe pass on the wrong message. Their true stories are seen as mere myths. They are not considered to be of ultimate value.

To develop the nautical theme, I have heard many shipwrights scoffing at those sailors who rely solely on their satellite navigation systems without reference to their charts. Such sailors forget that their satnav gives them data from a fixed position on their boat (normally behind the keel) and that their boat is constantly moving through the water. As a result they are not aware of underwater rocks that can suddenly tear a hole in their boat when they thought they were in a safe place. They have been sailing "carefully" through an area where they know rocks exist, but by keeping an eye only on their satnav they have proceeded confidently to run into a rock.

So it is with parents who think they have it all sewn up as they tell Bible stories to children, thinking that their meaning is clear while in reality they are passing on another more sinister meaning. In other words, the nightmare for us as parents is that we think we know the story of faith, but we communicate a toxic faith. We need to be mindful of the scripture that says: "So, if you think you are standing firm, be careful that you don't fall!" (1 Corinthians 10:12).

The idea of clear meaning is not clear in itself. (BW)

There are times when as parents we fail to question our instruments and charts. We sail blithely on, unaware that we are on the wrong track. We can even use the Bible for our own ends and tell stories that are not biblical, using the Bible to justify them. In different times, history records this to have happened, for example, when the church sanctioned the Holy Crusades against Muslims because of their occupation of the holy city of Jerusalem in the twelfth century. Christians then condoned a "holy war". Other examples are when Christian thinking upheld slavery, apartheid, or oppressive regimes. At an individual level, this is exactly what happens when parents become the sole interpreters of Scripture, or look exclusively to their own judgments. It can happen when the parent is the sole mediator of truth to the child. Maybe the child needs to learn to find their own discernment by discovering the layers of truth in the narrative for themselves.

> **I completely agree. Children should not be led in the direction that the parent wants, but rather should be given choices/questions offered by the parent. (BW)**

As a parent, the times when I have most doubted the Christian narrative have been when I am insecure or troubled. Personally I do not often doubt the existence of God, but I often question the means by which God's story has been transmitted through the Holy Scripture. At times, rather than seeing the Bible as a helpful chart, I have seen it as a collection of stories that have embodied an ancient patriarchal narrative that is comfortable with violence and prejudice. In the wrong hands, I know all too well that it can become a weapon of warfare to justify almost anything, rather than shining light on the pathway. When might I be using the Bible selectively to justify my own assumptions as opposed to correcting my biases? As a parent, might I be using

Scripture to gain compliance from my children as opposed to wrestling with it and reflecting on its meaning with them?

One occasion when I fear that I forced my own scriptural perspective on to my children was when I attempted to justify why our country had gone to war. I had been appalled by the way the United Nations was so ineffective in not preventing the Rwandan genocide in the 1990s. Stories were told about Hutu militia flagrantly arming young men with crude weapons and then proceeding to kill Tutsi villagers while United Nations personnel stood by, armed but forbidden to intervene. I recall telling my sons that authority does not carry the sword in vain (see Romans 13:4), implying that the United Nations should have intervened with force and taken a political stance. I went further and defended the ensuing violence when the UK government commissioned war on Middle Eastern countries. These wars were to dominate British politics for a long time. Later, I learned that Tony Blair, the prime minister at that time, made exactly the same mistake by believing he needed to intervene in overseas politics because of the apparent failure of UN strategy in Rwanda. I guess the only difference between Blair and me was that he had the power to direct and implement a policy for war, whereas I merely supported it and used scriptural justification for my thinking. This I now deeply regret, in that I had effectively taught my sons to condone warfare with little critique.

I recall a conversation with Dad after reading *Of Mice and Men* (by John Steinbeck) about whether we would have shot Lenny. I came to the conclusion that I would, but Dad said he wouldn't. It made me think. (BW)

Nonetheless, as a parent I always endeavoured to tell the Bible to the boys in ways they could hear, hoping they would get the true story. In reality, I resorted to using every genre of story available, every medium of communication, any story that grabbed attention. I fear that when I did this without care, it was because I wanted my world view to be supported. I wanted the Bible to back up my assumptions.

Thinking about reading myths with children as a means of telling truth

One of my greatest fears is that no true story exists. The only story available for humans is but a fragment of the true story, and even that is only a shard of truth that is likely to do damage rather than shed light. If all that is left from the one true story is devolved legends that are diluted into myths, then everything is relative and all is but a pursuit of the wind.

I don't have much to add about the negative side of storytelling – apart from protesting at Dad's use of the word "myth" in a negative light. For me a myth is always an attempted step towards truth. I always find it sad when people become affronted when the Bible is called a myth by its detractors. I understand that the intention is derisory. But that is just because those same detractors dismiss the term myth too! A myth is a story that attempts to explain the divine; a story that holds a truth that cannot be contained by a mere accounting of the facts. What else are Jesus' parables or the story of creation other than myths that point beyond themselves

to something so much more: God's long and complicated
love letter to the world? (NW)

As a parent reading to children at night, there were times when
I feared that the Bible would not be seen to be as interesting
as the other stories I told. In fact, I always felt that my sons
were gently humouring me if I tacked on biblical narrative to
the many myths and poems and legends I told at night – they
were humouring me in accepting the biblical text that had
been added to the more interesting story. I sensed that their
unwritten script was, "Dad needs to get his Bible bit in, so
let's listen so that we can get back to *The Rogues of Alwyn*" (or
whatever we were reading).

I think what Dad means to say is that occasionally he
would feel guilty for getting wrapped up in the story
we were reading and try to "ham fist" the conversation
back to something morally improving… or biblical. My
thoughts on this are simple: the deep conversations will
arise either way, whether from a story about dragons or
one about God. The only bad conversations are forced
ones. For more on this subject check Dad's abortive effort
to set up a monthly family hour when a poorly inspired
reading of *The 7 Habits of Highly Effective Families* (by
Stephen Covey) inspired derision from us. This book did
not prove to be highly effective or long-lived. No offence,
Dad, but the idea of having a business-style meeting with
your family, where everyone shares positive ideas and
grievances, was one of your worst yet. (JW)

I tried to examine this academically when I observed that my children greatly favoured made-up stories over the biblical narrative. By making this distinction I am not saying that made-up stories do not contain truth, nor that the Bible has no myth in it, but rather I am saying that those stories were clearly not written as truth were more interesting than the Bible, with its clearly authoritative gravitas.

> See my reference to Schiller from earlier in this book.
> I can't really tell you why, but I've always preferred fiction to non-fiction. I still read novels every day, but very rarely finish a "serious book" – in the same way I love travelling but always skim travel writing. (JW)

What I decided to do was to opt for the pragmatic route. I was not going to read the Bible to my children for big chunks of time, because they were not particularly interested in this. I read stories they enjoyed. So I used stories that I liked and they liked. I reasoned with myself that biblical truth was contained in all great stories.

> I think we preferred fictitious story because it was written better. If you look at the gospels as stories, they do not have the extra detail into certain character portrayal that fiction books provide. That is not their purpose. That's because the Bible is not a story book in the same way. It can't be. (BW)

Can we read Christian themes from secular children's stories?

To test the assumption that all good stories are versions of God's big story, I researched and wrote two articles that explored theological themes in children's literature. I wanted to apply theological reflection to the stories I was reading to the boys. Did the secular and post-Christian stories that I was reading echo the Bible? Was the Bible a repository of the true story and were those biblical themes accessible in all good stories? My hope was that all good literature was appealing because it was able to communicate God's truth, and that the great themes of forgiveness, hope, atonement, creation, and redemption (to name but a few) could be traced through all great literature.

> From my current experience of teaching primary school children, I don't often finish a story unless it's a good one and captures their imagination. They want to be entertained. The Bible is read for many reasons, including fiction. Yet fiction is also about entertainment. I think this needs to be reflected on when reading the Bible with kids. St Paul is not J. K. Rowling. (BW)

The first academic article I wrote on this subject explored the theme of atonement in children's literature (Worsley, 2004) and the sequel investigated the theme of grace in children's literature (Worsley, 2010a). Both articles compared the mythical books we were reading at night with the doctrine I was teaching at theological college (where I was a lecturer in contextual theology). My inner exploration was to find out whether reading good children's fantasy and drawing out the biblical or theological themes from it was as good as (or better than) reading the Bible.

Let me explain further by discussing these two themes of atonement and grace considered in those two articles.

The theme of atonement in mythical children's literature

The first article I wrote was entitled "Popularised Atonement Theory Reflected in Children's Literature" and in it I set out to refer to four works of children's literature: *The Lion, the Witch and the Wardrobe*, the first of the Narnia Chronicles by C. S. Lewis (1950); *The Lord of the Rings* by J. R. R. Tolkien (1954); *The Druid of Shannara* by Terry Brooks (1991); and the Harry Potter stories that had been completed before the turn of the century by J. K. Rowling (1997, 1998, 1999, 2000). None of these books was written with the intention of echoing any overt Christian atonement narrative (with the probable exception of the Narnia Chronicles), but they do contain a strong Christian world view, complete with the outworking of salvation by characters who operate as alternative Christ figures. The article traced four atonement theories seen in these children's books.

Taking each model of atonement in turn – sacrifice (model 1), the demands of justice (model 2), the decisive victory (model 3), and the act of love (model 4) – I attempted to demonstrate how these four fictional works evidenced aspects of classic Christian atonement theory. In making such connections, I did not impute any cognitive religious belief system to the original storytellers. I examined each of the works with respect to the four atonement theories by referring to (1) the Christ figure identified, (2) the task of salvation, and (3) the means of atonement.

I concluded that this brief exploration of atonement theory in children's literature gave me grounds for hope as well as reflection. It suggested that spirituality was finding its own route into the modern subconscious and that classic atonement theories were present in some of the major works of fiction. However, it also gave me a fresh awareness that old ideas of the atonement were still very prevalent. If Christ was portrayed as a bait that can catch and hang the devil (as in Lewis's *The Lion, the Witch and the Wardrobe*, where Aslan deceived the White Witch), what are the ethical terms of reference, and in what ways can salvation be won without deception? It seems that only Lily Potter had found a way through this dilemma by showing unconditional love in overcoming malevolence. I took note of Howard Marshall's assertion (1992) that, just as New Testament writers were "more concerned with the nature of salvation than the precise way in which it has been achieved", so children's literature preserves the story of salvation without detailing how.

I know that there has been some reductionist Christian backlash against certain children's books that are seen to be dangerous in some way, be that *His Dark Materials* by Pullman (one of my favourites and yet wonderfully subversive) or even laughably the Harry Potter books (which, as Dad has pointed out, advance a moral theology of sacrifice). I take issue with anyone who seeks to ban books of any kind. Surely it can't be right to only allow your children to read something because you feel it pushes a certain set of ideas that you are comfortable with. This is propaganda. I agree with the quote attributed to Frederick Douglass (whose poster adorned my school's English class): "Once you learn to read, you will be forever free." Reading is radical and we insult the critical capacity of young people if we do not allow them to make their own judgments. (JW)

The theme of grace in mythical children's literature

My second article examined the concept of grace, and was entitled "Children's Literature as Implicit Religion: The Concept of Grace Unpacked" (2010).

It noted how the Christian concept of grace is widely explored in children's literature and is a hallmark of contemporary spirituality found beyond the walls of the church. For the purposes of the article, grace was discussed by way of these hallmarks, identified by a wider look at the literature that focused on grace. These were three aspects of grace seen as:

- forgiveness (without a demand for justice);
- moving on (without vengeance); and
- extravagant offering.

These three hallmarks of grace were noted as being identifiable human virtues that are in some ways beyond the grasp of most humans and yet widely affirmed within contemporary spirituality. They are marks of an implicit religion to which the human spirit testifies without a religious context.

As in my previous article on atonement, this one on grace focused on children's literature as being the place where religion leaves its residual mark in ways that are implicit rather than intentional. The writers chosen were the same as for the earlier article.

At the end of this study I concluded that by retracing the footsteps of grace through children's literature, it had become apparent that the very aspect of the books that made them particularly compelling was grace. Children are interested in justice and yet love grace, and often bring it out of unexpected places. The movement of grace is the touch of beauty that teaches us to live.

Having written earlier about atonement in children's literature (2004), I now observed that grace was less interested in explanations of grand schemes for atonement and explanations of redemption. I now sensed that grace went beyond justice seen in formulated atonement theories and offered something more than a sensible or cognitively balanced solution to the presence of evil. Grace broke out of any theory, because it was not anxious to justify itself. It was only concerned in acting justly, even if this was not widely understood. This is a core feature of implicit religion. I concluded: "It is therefore no surprise that the themes of grace are what keep some of our most popular authors high in the attention of children and in the regard of those who draw on the insights of children."

So, is it a cop-out to read fantasy books to children when desiring to pass on the true story? Have I been part of a generation of adults that caused the Oxford English dictionary in 2016 to say that the new and most used word in the English language was "post-truth"? Has the authoritative truth of the Bible been relativized by indulging in myth?

To the best of my ability, as I have read fiction to my children, I have always said that these books contain truth, that fictional stories are interesting not just because they are well told but because they are true. But maybe on a cold night when the winds of secularism are blowing and when only a more strident form of confessional faith is whistling round the land, I ask myself if I have taken the easy route. What if my sons do not trace back the biblical themes in fantasy literature to the revealed Word of God? Will I then have become guilty of trivializing the Scriptures?

Only time will tell.

> I think Dad is right in that everything has a truth of sorts. Like Plato's world of the forms, there is truth in everything – just varying degrees from its truest form. Like Jesus being the truest form of man. (BW)

For the time being, I am content that we had many a great evening reading and chatting about life, our conversations inspired by the text we were reading. It would clearly have been religiously abusive to force a biblical pattern of reading on to the boys and it would have been dull for me, as well as dishonouring to the Bible. What I tried to do was make connections and to facilitate theological discussion.

And of course there are many myths at work in secular culture. In fact, the virtual is often more powerful than what is real. This causes confusion in many cultural tales of truth. In the twenty-first century, gender and sexuality, faith, and ethnicity are becoming commodities of choice that can be changed in real time as well as in narrative. Enhancing reality in the digital world allows a widening range of engagement and fresh options of behaviour. New ways of thinking are emerging in fantasy play and in real time, and in it all the distinction between myth and truth is becoming increasingly blurred. The academic world is now more aware of postmodern criticism, with its suspicions of power. It is in this world that our children need to learn to weave the thread of faith without being seduced into fundamentalism or coerced into secularist relativism. Our job as parents is to give them the tools that can draw on faith with skill and confidence, understanding myth and sensing the power of God's true story within it.

The habit of reading myths with children

I can recall one morning, when our boys were still at primary school, listening to one of their favourite story tapes over breakfast. It was a tape of a dozen mythological stories, each lasting about five minutes. Most of them were gripping fairy tales (like *Beauty and the Beast*, *Rapunzel*, or *Rumpelstiltskin*). Of this selection, a couple were comical moral stories (like Aesop's *The Fox and the Crow* or *The Little Red Hen*) and a couple were Bible stories. I remember this well because the Bible stories were about Joseph and his multicoloured coat and Jonah and the whale. My concern at the time was that the tape was mixing up two genres that I wished to keep separate. It was positioning Bible stories in the same genre as fantasy stories. Was the tape confusing the children, or was it me, as a religious believer, who was confusing them?

In my mind, biblical literature had a distinctive status and I wished to tell Bible stories with a degree of awe. I would normally tell the Bible story after a prayer and then we would reflect on it. However, for the boys to hear the Bible story told within a hermeneutic of entertainment (as being merely an interesting story) was somehow offensive to me. I needed to reflect and ask myself what was going on here. In the end, I did what many parents do, in that I went with the flow. In other words I was pragmatic and I allowed the stories on the tape to be heard without offering initial comment. I felt that my options were either to play the heavy-handed parent or to be the reflective parent. The heavy-handed parent would forbid the tape being played and be prosaic by objecting to the mixing of genres by saying that Bible stories had a truth that the other stories on the tape did not have (something the children would not have understood). Alternatively, the reflective parent would let the tape be heard and look for ways to open the conversation of biblical authority at a later stage.

In the event, I did ask the boys about the tape many years later and they considered my question amusing. Did I think that by giving the Bible the high status of God's Word this meant everything within it was to be understood literally? Did I think that a large fish really did swallow up Jonah and then spit him out, and that a gourd grew up overnight to protect him, only to shrivel up immediately after a worm had bitten into it?

> I think what I got from this view of a blur between the Bible and other stories was a critical one. I think I still hold an ambiguous view of the Bible, with its variety of poetry, prose, allegory, and so on, and I do fear my cynicism of religion. But I am aware of my cynicism. (BW)

My question as a parent was to consider how to approach the genre of Scripture without being heavy-handed, prosaic, or literalist. I wanted to reflect on whether it was possible for a large fish to swallow a man, as in the story of Jonah, but not to have to conclude that this literal way of understanding was the only way of interpretation. In fact, as I stayed with the story of Jonah for a longer period, I wanted to see many other interpretations. I began to see the humour of the prophet telling a story against himself. I saw the wide-angled theology that portrayed the sailors in the boat as having more awareness of God than the preacher Jonah. I began to understand that this story was amazingly well constructed to make a theological point (that God is far more gracious than he is vengeful). But how could I bring such thinking to little boys who were hearing it as a mythical story alongside many other obviously cultural myths?

My answer was to relax and let God be the parent of my children. In fact, as time went by, I became more comfortable with the complexity of narrative genres. Stories can be heard on many different levels and can be understood by different age groups simultaneously.

It was this way of thinking that helped me to work out how to handle the question of Father Christmas.

Should we tell our children about Father Christmas?

In the church that we attended when our boys were small, it was not uncommon for someone to say in a loud stage whisper that Father Christmas was not real. I think this was because there was a fear that children might be confused by the make-believe stories surrounding the authentic birth narrative of the Christ child. I remember one well-meaning character who felt that it was important to explain that the man behind the big white beard who was driving the fake sleigh down the road was not the real Father Christmas. This person possibly thought the boys could not see that behind the Christmas lights on the cardboard sides of the red sleigh was a Land Rover and that the wheels were clearly visible behind the fake runners. He was worried that children would initially believe everything we told them and subsequently reject everything we told them.

Around this time, a newspaper article covered the story of how some parents wanted to sue an independent church pastor for going into a school assembly and pronouncing that Father Christmas was not real, but that Jesus was the real deal. He had caused an outcry and some parents wanted him banned from school because he was destroying the romance of Christmas for the children. In the event, what the pastor had actually done was to have a quiz entitled "The Real Meaning of Christmas" and had given a number of "true or false?" questions. Some Year 6 children had gone home distraught on hearing that Father Christmas did not exist.

I used to cite this as a case study to my students (Anglican ordinands training to be vicars in the Church of England) and get them to discuss it. There would always be a wide cross section of views, ranging from those who thought it best not to confuse children with mixed messages about truth to those who were quite comfortable with the thought that children are able to work it out for themselves over a period of time. If I were to simplify their discussions, I would say that they broadly fell into two camps: those who had a literal insight into reality and those who had a more poetic insight. Some students perceived children to be static in their thinking and understanding, and others felt that they are developmental beings who have a spectrum of understanding.

Whatever the outcome of such a class discussion, I always insisted on some background reading to be considered in terms of how a child grows up. Beginning with Jean Piaget in the 1920s and progressing through the work of James Fowler, who applied developmental theory to considering how faith grows, we would look at the movement of cognition within a child. In overview terms, Fowler (1981) offered a stage developmental theory that is consistent for interpreting the way children and adults understand faith realities. He suggested that children develop through a phase of mythical realism into to a time of reality testing until they are able to hold several perspectives simultaneously.

> I remember having to help Dad type up a journal article he was writing about Fowler, which was a comparison with some German theologian whose name I can't remember. I remember looking at Fowler's stages and placing myself in one, only to have a conversation with Dad, who placed me in a separate stage. I remember thinking that the reason I didn't like it was that I saw the stages as hierarchical. I wanted that independence from influence of parents. Now I realize parental influence is a given. All we can do is be aware of it and try to walk our own path, be that similar or different from that of our parents. (BW)

When it comes to considering whether or not to treat Father Christmas as real, it is not just a question of parental ethics. It is about "going with the flow" of childhood development. Father Christmas is a creation that works during the stage when a child is unable to distinguish myth from reality, when the child is making sense of the world through story. The story is like a great flowing river and the child is immersed in the middle of it as he or she floats along. At this stage of development, parents need to be able to collude with their children's intuitions and projected realities. In these early days of childhood, Father Christmas will exist alongside the Tooth Fairy and the Easter Bunny... and Jesus and God the Father and God the Holy Spirit. Reality testing will come later.

As the child exists within this world of wonder, the parent needs to be able to enjoy the child's world, not correct it. In due course the child will invariably move through to a more developed way of thinking. They will become the "young scientist" as they scrutinize everything for reality and myth, wanting to reduce everything to concrete certainties. At this point, many children will be suspicious of anything that cannot be evidenced and will be fearful that adults are hatching webs of false reality to con them.

For the Christian parent, this is a time to have fun and to trust God. To the question "Does Father Christmas exist?" we might answer, "Let's discuss it. What do you think?"

For ourselves, in our family of small boys, the complex question "Should we tell our children the truth about Father Christmas?" was answered by accepting the cultural myth as it was presented at school and by adding to it in the home. I had come from a background where Father Christmas had no currency whatsoever, but my wife could remember the joy of hanging up a stocking on Christmas Eve and hearing the poem

"The Night Before Christmas" read as a ritual. At Christmas time her story was further enhanced by a favourite uncle (or so she thinks) stealing into the house at midnight dressed in red and sporting a fine beard. In the early years of her life she really believed he was in fact Father Christmas. As a result she loved Christmas and spent many years working out how to discover whether this mysterious man in red was the universal Santa Claus or an elaborate hoax. Interestingly, her own coming to faith in God took place at this stage in her life when she was still "reality testing" for Father Christmas.

Therefore at Christmas we decided to adopt a similar practice. I, or a visitor to the home, would bring the stockings that had been hung by the fireplace up to the bedrooms. The effort of doing so was normally wasted, as the boys were sound asleep. "Father Christmas" would creep into each room and leave the loaded stocking by the appropriate bed. However, as the years went by, the boys began to set traps for their midnight visitor. One Christmas night I found that a trip wire had been cunningly stretched from the foot of the bed to the door. Another Christmas, they worked out that it was difficult for a fat man to come down a thin chimney flue, but they theorized that it was done by a magical action invoked by holding the nose before descent. Yet another Christmas problem arose over the fact that Father Christmas had consumed the glass of whisky left out for him, but had forgotten to take the juicy carrot left for Rudolf. I had no answer for this!

Many years later, I discussed these antics with the boys. The oldest said that he had kept the story going so that the youngest would continue to have as much fun as he had had. He also said that a vague fear had been present in him that if he blew the story open, this might foreshadow the end of getting presents. Therefore, as a wise pragmatist, he had kept quiet. More tellingly, when asked as a teenager about the reality testing between Father Christmas and God, he thought this quite amusing. He said that there was no comparison. When I talked about Father Christmas I always had a twinkle in my eye. It was clear to him that I was in "storytelling mode". He said, "When you talked about God, it was something you did all the time, on walks, at dinner, etc. You clearly believed in God. When we wanted your attention, you would go into 'theological mode'. We knew you really believed in God. Our question was not whether Father Christmas was real, but whether you were right in thinking God was real."

I have always been a great believer. Funnily enough I don't have a traumatic memory of the renunciation of my belief in Father Christmas. Perhaps I was always fairly content with that one. I do remember believing for years that my dad had a button on his car's dashboard that would make it fly and another that would make it into a submarine. It was only remembering this childish but serious belief as an adult that caused me to question it. But rather than feeling betrayed by the deception, if anything I was pretty impressed both by Dad's gambit and by my own innocent abandonment to fantasy. I think it is good to believe in stories, even when they're silly. The dark and dangerous side to this is the point where belief is allowed to be unquestioned or is left unmitigated by experience. I vividly remember telling my dad that if I believed enough I would be able to fly. I could jump out of my bedroom window

> just like Peter Pan. I think this scared him a little – enough
> to challenge me at least – but I still hope to be open to
> ridiculous magic. After all, "Those who don't believe in
> magic will never find it."[4] (JW)

This imaginative co-mixture between reality and fantasy served us well. On holiday, we would tell long invented stories about the places we were visiting. One year we booked a holiday cottage on the island of Shuna off the west coast of Scotland. The first night there we "discovered" a bottle stuffed up the chimney. In the bottle was a message from a former dweller in that house who had lived there two centuries before. It was encrusted with age, partly burnt, and reeking of smoke. It instructed us to set out to find treasure. This treasure trail lasted for the whole week, until we arrived at the far end of the island and discovered a vast cache of food and drink and treasure in the form of age-related toys.

> I remember during one trip to Shuna being told that a
> helicopter had dropped off a gift for me. Well, at least that
> was what I was told. From the sniggers from my brothers,
> I soon thought otherwise. (BW)

Were we playing with fragile minds and unformed world views? I think not. What we were doing as parents was re-entering the lost world of childish imagination and rediscovering the treasures forgotten by adults.

Yet I still reflect deeply on the nature of truth and myth. How might we ever know truth if we are to behold God? How might we

---

4   Roald Dahl, *The Minpins* (Jonathan Cape, 1991).

perceive truth, given our fragile intellect and perceptions? And then how are we to communicate this complex phenomenon to our children as they develop through a period of mythical reality into a period of literalism and then poetic reality?

On a good day, I trusted that God would reveal himself through the frailties of language and storytelling. On a bad day, I dreaded that I had merely confounded truth and mixed it with myth, destroying any chance of my children believing in God.

For discussion

Section A

- What do you think constitutes the true story of faith?
- As a parent, what are the personal stories from the story of faith that most influence you?
- What are the ways of reading the Bible with children that you consider to be inadequate and what are the better ways of reading it with children?

Section B

- What are the differences between true story, myth, and legend? How can you tell?
- How does a child learn to tell the difference between fact and fiction?
- What other great Christian themes (as well as atonement and grace) find their way into children's literature?

CHAPTER 2

Going on Adventures and Making Memories

(A) When We Went on Adventures

He will go on before the Lord, in the spirit and power of Elijah, to turn the hearts of the parents to their children.

(Luke 1:17)

Life is an adventure. It begins with the exit from the womb, then the discovery that we are different from our mother. It continues with the realization that we have the ability to influence our surroundings. We discover that we can get around under our own steam as life opens up new possibilities. This adventure is initially accompanied by the parent, who on a good day is the coach or the safety net, but on a bad day is the policeman or the judge. Growing up calls for new relationships to be navigated as new identities are formed between the parent and the child.

At birth, the infant begins a journey through life that will be filled with opportunities and challenges. In the beginning, we all learn how to communicate in order to have our needs met and influence our surroundings. We learn how to value praise and to succeed, from the moment the toilet is used correctly through to when complex and dexterous skills are achieved. Initially, parents reward the growing child for achievement and protect them from dangers. Later, the child discovers his or her own motivation and means of being rewarded.

At the beginning of life the child will be stimulated to try out new things, encouraged by those in the family home. Initially these encouragers are parents, grandparents, or siblings. These are the people who first sow the seeds for adventure and enable it to happen.

One of the key adventures in life is the journey of faith. This journey will be the landscape against which all other journeys are mapped. As we have discussed in the previous chapter, faith is the true story that provides the reference points against which the young life can be plotted.

I feel that this chapter is inseparable from the one before. Our adventures were always us enacting our own stories. Mostly the reason for the adventures was to find a good spot for a story. If you are serious about telling stories then you need to be serious about going on adventures. In fact, they perform vital checks and balances against each other. If you only go on adventures I think you are in danger of living a distinctly unreflected life. I wonder if this leads to what is often termed as being an "adrenaline junkie". One constantly seeks evermore dangerous adventures without ever really working out why.

However, if you merely read stories, then you are in danger of becoming the sentimental armchair adventurer to whom danger and discomfort seem exhilarating. You have to feel the thousandth midge bite, smell the stink of feet after weeks of wet boots, or feel the shock and pain after falling from height onto rocks to be jolted into reality.

For me this has always been the saving grace for both our storytelling and our adventures. Each one provided a realistic framework for the other. Storytelling connected us with other people's adventures and the need for them, and helped us to work out why we did our own, while our own experience of adventure reminded us that it often wasn't a comfortable or pleasant experience. (NW)

When we who are parents begin to reflect on how we pass on our faith, it is crucial that we identify good stories of adventure that can help our growing children to think about faith. We also need to provide opportunities for adventure that will stretch their imagination and their abilities without them being endangered. As a parent, I reflected on how I might:

- identify stories of adventure that build faith; and
- create opportunities for adventure that would help faith to grow.

Identifying stories that build faith

The Bible contains a store of adventure stories that can excite the growing child and can become the overarching stories behind all stories. They are the big stories of how God created the world and then became a human being in order to save the world. At a secondary level there are the classic stories of God's people escaping from Egypt and entering the Promised Land, and then of the early church beginning to tell the story of Jesus around the Mediterranean. Within these metanarratives are many smaller personal stories of courage told about Noah, Abraham, Isaac, Jacob, Moses, and so on – many of whom are recorded in Hebrews 11 in the "catalogue of fame". These stories have been told in different contexts throughout history and can be the keys that unlock other stories. Of great note is the Exodus story just mentioned, about how the children of Israel managed to escape from Egypt. It is a story of freedom that has inspired the poor throughout the ages, particularly nineteenth-century slaves in the West Indies and twentieth-century Christians oppressed in South Africa.

By telling the story in a safe place that allows for reflection, we enable the story to germinate and grow. The reflected story becomes the idea for a plan of action. The plan becomes a lived reality when it is enacted.

So it was for me as a child visiting my grandparents in Edinburgh and being allowed the freedom of wandering from the home. I had heard stories of adventurers who discovered new lands, and one day I had the opportunity to become one. Near my grandparents' home in Morningside, Edinburgh, was a stream called the Braid Burn. I loved the idea of calling a stream a "burn". I wondered where the burn started. I had been taught that streams either flow down from a hillside or bubble up from an underground source. The idea of finding the source of the Braid Burn was fascinating to me, but so too was where it might lead to. Would it cut through a valley and broaden out into a river, or would it go underground? This was to become an adventure based on imagination and encouraged by my grandmother. Looking back as an adult I wrote a poem entitled "Where Does the Braid Burn Go?"

The adventurer planned a route his grandpa never took,
So packed his bag and cut his sandwiches
And set out down the loan, along the crescent,
Turning right beside the Burn.

It was a bright fresh day in August, untouched by school or adult,
Focused just on finding out the stream's wet path,
Through the meadow, round allotments,
Down a gully and flowing by the mountain.

The traveller stopped at midday when the sun was high,
Cheese butties tasting like a monarch's lunch,
Plastic tinted water sparkling like a Perrier
And wonder, future, purpose filled the air.

After lunch the stream went underground,
Don't know where or how. And the youth
Climbed the mountain back to Grandma's house,
Leaving adventure in the young boy's soul.

My chief delight in writing this poem was to realize that adventure had been unlocked when I was still a child. Looking back, I can see that my grandparents had encouraged my speculations about the Braid Burn and then helped me to prepare to investigate and explore. As a child I discovered that I could find out things that were not known by myself or others. This was true in exploring the physical geography of my surroundings and it was also true in exploring the mysteries of God. As an inquisitive child I remember thinking that I might find out new insights about God in the Bible.

Acquiring new information breeds confidence. It allows growing children to discover that not only can they survive but they can also shape the world. I recall this feeling when, as a pre-adolescent looking out of my grandmother's warm sitting room, I worked out how to face the rain and sleet without getting wet. Rather than remaining trapped and cocooned by the fireside on a wet day, I dreamed of building a shelter. I imagined what it would have been like to be a member of the Israelite tribe that was forced to travel in the Sinai desert for forty years. How did they survive? What happened if it rained? Where did they go to the toilet? I wondered what it would feel like to be a refugee child who was forced to flee from their homeland because of war.

I hatched a plan to learn how to weather the storm. I gathered a tarpaulin and old cushions, and considered how to adapt the garden furniture into a shelter that might be called home. This also became the subject of a poem that I wrote as an adult, looking back at the point when childhood imagination developed into adventure.

The Storm Is Coming

The gathering storm cloud is welcome to the lad,
Who has endured the summer's strength,
Collecting for the storm.

Now he brings out all his store;
A plastic sheet to cover up the garden bench,
Some bricks to hold it down,
Cushions from the sofa which may go into the den,
Because the storm is coming.

He waits impatiently for the first fat drops
That will not come.
He hears a tap upon his fragile lodge,
Is glad to take the biscuit and the drink, and
Then it comes!
O bliss, the long-awaited storm.

These early personal forays into adventure, encouraged by my grandparents, were the bedrock of memory that allowed my own parenting style to include adventures. Subsequently, as a father I felt that my job was not to provide the adventure but rather to provide the conditions in which an adventure might take place. If my children were to wonder and explore, then they would desire the adventure and would bring their own investigation and preparation to the task. The adventure would not be an adult project but one that came from my children's imagination. It seemed to me that my task was to stimulate their natural wonder.

Thinking about how to encourage adventure, I reflected on the proverb "You can lead a horse to water but you cannot make it drink". My fear was that as a parent I might create the right environment for adventure, but the children would not avail themselves of the opportunity. However, I had also heard it said that you can lead a horse to water but you cannot make it drink, *but you can add salt to its oats*.

It was this philosophy that inspired me. My role as a parent was to create a thirst for adventure and to develop the appetite for adventure. How was this to be done? How was salt to be added to the oats of life?

Creating opportunities for adventure that will help faith to grow

The thirst for adventure is created in stages by building on early success. Many children do not like going camping because they find the ground is harder than their beds at home or because they find themselves cold and uncomfortable. They might also discover that their parents do not enjoy themselves as they brave conditions they were not prepared for. If the adventure fails or does not gain interest, it might not be repeated.

The way round this is to envisage the trip, live out the adventure, long before it ever happens. So I set out to plan adventures with my children that they would treasure as memories. These adventures were to be combined with opportunities to discuss faith.

Our first adventure: in Farmer Bettison's field

My first curacy was in an ex-mining town in north Nottinghamshire. The church I served had been built by coal miners from stones quarried from the deep pits in the area. When Ruth and I arrived in the 1990s as parents to three boys – a seven-year-old, a five-year-old, and an infant – the mines had been shut down, and unemployment was common. However, there were still some old-fashioned farms operating on the hillsides and there were quarry pits. Some of these were owned by farmers who occasionally came to church, and it was with one of these farmers that I began to plan how to create an adventure with the boys. Farmer Bettison was the introverted farmer who suggested I camp in his upper field with our little family.

We had been reading a wonderful story each night. It was entitled *The Little Wooden Horse*, a tale of a toy horse who travelled the world to find his fame and fortune. When this story finished we went on to another story of travel called *I Am David*, an insightful tale of a small boy who escaped from an enclosure to travel on his own across Europe. Both stories described the hardships of travelling alone and being beset by difficulties: of camping rough, of keeping warm, and of finding sufficient food to survive. Each night in the winter of 1994, we read these books and prayed, thinking of survival and adventure as we reflected on the story. So we came up with the idea of going on a trip into the unknown. This was where Farmer Bettison's field featured.

One Friday night after school, we set out into the wilds. I had one small boy sitting on my shoulders and the other two in either hand. We crossed a stile at the back of school, climbed a hill, cut back through the woods, and walked through a valley near the quarry. It appeared that we were heading out into the unknown, uncertain as to where we were going. It was not clear to the boys where our next crust would be found.

As it happened, I had gained permission to cross the Bettison farmland and to enter his quarry. I had buried small caches of food along the way, enabling us to snack as we travelled, until we arrived in a field that the boys had never seen before. In that field, we discovered some tents, a Trangia cooking stove, and more food. We soon set about erecting the tents and preparing a hot meal. It was all an act of discovery and adventure. Then, as the sun set, we were greeted by a fine sight: Ruth approaching with a rucksack filled with sleeping bags. She stayed long enough to ensure that the travellers were settled down and comfortable before disappearing from where she'd arrived. (In the event, it transpired that the field in which we were camping was only a quarter of a mile from our home, although we had tramped several miles to find it.)

Before we went to sleep, we took time lying on our backs to observe the night sky. We became acquainted with the Plough, and I taught them how to work out the North Star (by following the back edge of "the saucepan" upwards). Noticing the sky alerted us to the shooting stars that skim the atmosphere.

Then, as we became sleepy, we thanked God for the day, for school, for our warm sleeping bags, for our tent, and for the food we had eaten. The "thank you" prayers were followed by "please" prayers. "Please" prayers were for those things that seemed important to us: the people at school who were lonely or unkind, the sad people caught up in warfare or poverty, the hope that we could treasure moments of reality (like this) in our hearts for ever. We all slept like logs, warm and happy even though the rain fell heavily on our tent and then a light frost encrusted the ground. We had managed to enjoy camping in March.

From that successful experience of the outdoors, we began to plan more trips. We became good at knowing what to pack (we mustn't forget the toilet roll) and what not to pack (we didn't need heavy tins of baked beans). One thing we always packed was a small cross, which we'd put out at prayer time to make an outdoor chapel.

Making adventure a habit

From camping in Farmer Bettison's field, we graduated to the harder stuff. Birthday presents became small rucksacks, and the gear for the trip was shared round in our packs as we went on longer walks. The most desired Christmas presents were high-quality sleeping bags that could keep us warm at −20°. And interestingly, the prayer habit from going camping became embedded as well. Impromptu prayers gave way to using compline booklets, and these became so well used that they fell apart and had to be replaced. (Compline is the last office said in a monastery before lights out and the "greater silence", and they contain a minimalist liturgy, with set readings and prayers for the end of the day.) We would take it in turns to lead compline and whoever led the service would be responsible for allocating the task of reading the Bible or of leading the intercessions.

Other overnight camps included scaling the Dark Peak in Derbyshire, using a Canadian canoe to "overnight" on the River Trent, or going to the island of Shuna.

Going to Shuna

I discovered the island of Shuna when I was on a conference for Scripture Union staff workers, at which we were sharing our prospects for the approaching summer vacation. One of my colleagues mentioned an island off the west coast of Scotland on which a few cottages were available for rent. They were basic homes heated by log fires and lit at night by paraffin lamps and candles as they weren't connected to electricity, phone lines, or the internet. Peaty-coloured water was pumped from the island springs. To get to the island a motor launch would collect guests from a remote pier and return them again at the end of the trip. Most enticingly, a small landing craft was included with the cost of the cottage, as long as users attended some basic training to ensure they understood the vagaries of the local currents and tidal flow.

We discussed whether this might be the sort of holiday adventure we could enjoy. Could we live like the ancient crofters in a candlelit cottage? Could we cut our own firewood to keep warm in the evenings? Could we take enough food to survive for a fortnight? Might we learn to catch fish or trap rabbits? Would we be expert enough to handle the landing craft, abiding by the rules of wearing life jackets and so on? This discussion became highly involved as we were drawn into the adventure and we began to create detailed kit lists and agree responsibilities for life in a croft.

In the event, we fell in love with Shuna, as it was a place that provided sufficient challenges without being too uncomfortable. We learned to cut wood using bow saws and hatchets. We discovered that water could be pure and drinkable even if it was peat-stained. We learned how to catch mackerel and to gut them and cook them fresh. We also built an underground oven using rocks and peat, and had a bread-making competition. When the weather was rough we sat by our fire and played board games. When it was dry we had treasure hunts, canoe races, fishing expeditions, and night hikes. There was plenty to do and we all shared in the experience, ending each day with a compline prayer lit by candles before bedtime.

Recalling those stories of adventure by "ritual and by rock stacks"

The Old Testament is a collection of books that all tell the adventure story of how God was faithful to his people the Israelites. It is also the story of how they learned to trust God. It describes their early origins, their movement from being a travelling people who became enslaved through to when they became settled in a land that God provided for them. Some of the key moments in that story are when they initially cross over the Red Sea to escape slavery and then later when they enter the Promised Land by crossing the River Jordan. Both of these boundary crossings are referred to time and again in the narrative of the Old Testaments books. They were told in public worship and in family devotions, in order to remind the next generation of the mighty deeds of God (see Psalm 78:1–7).

In the Old Testament, a key part of remembering these stories was *ritual* and another was *setting up memorial standing stones* (or "rock stacks"). The key ritual of escape from Egypt was remembered in the Passover meal (which was to develop for Christians into the Lord's Supper). The adventure of crossing over the Jordan was famously relived by getting stones from the river bed and making them into a memorial.

When the whole nation had finished crossing the
Jordan, the LORD said to Joshua, "Choose twelve men
from among the people, one from each tribe, and tell
them to take up twelve stones from the middle of the
Jordan, from right where the priests are standing, and
carry them over with you and put them down at the
place where you stay tonight." ... [And Joshua said]
"These stones are to be a memorial to the people of
Israel for ever."

(Joshua 4:1–3, 7)

As human beings we seek meaning and we mark memories by telling the big story of faith or the personal stories of our lives. Our personal adventures can be recalled in our conversations, or by photos or objects. So it is that we capture the good stories of our life of faith told out in the family history. We tell those stories at Christmas when we settle down to a good meal, and we tell them at other family gatherings. Sometimes the retelling of the stories is embellished, with different versions being created.

The other way that stories get told is through the "standing stones", the rock stacks of photographs, souvenirs, and gifts. Our house is cluttered with objects of huge significance that are of no financial worth. There is the tiny glass cross that looks as though it was made from icicles, which sat on Ruth's teenage study desk when I first met her. There is the fragment of a stick, broken and reset into the shape of a cross – a gift from a son after he had walked the Camino de Santiago. There is the most priceless sheep's head on a stick that was once a teenage boy's impression of a shaman, whom he named John the Baptist.

I like the idea of bits and pieces having meaning and memory. It's not materialism; it's symbology. (BW)

For discussion

- Do you agree that although you can lead a horse to water but not make it drink, *you can add salt to its oats*?
- Do you have biblical (or other) stories of adventure that you tell as a means of describing life?
- What rituals do you have as a family? What are they preserving?
- What are the rock stacks that you have in your family? What are they recalling?

(B) When We Created Nightmares (When Adventures became health and safety disasters)

Jephthah promised the Lord: "If you will give me victory over the Ammonites, I will burn as an offering the first person that comes out of my house to meet me, when I come back from the victory."
(Judges 11:30–31, GNB)

There seems to be a flip side to adventure, and that is foolishness. What might be termed brave might alternatively be called foolhardy when seen from a different perspective. Often it is history that decides, and even then history has a habit of shaping events to fit the narrative of the teller. So it was with the fearsome story of parental abuse told in the book of Judges, when Jephthah made a rash promise to God and ended up sacrificing his only child.

As parents, it is entirely possible to sacrifice our children on the altar of our ideology. The history of the nineteenth-century church missionary expansion is littered with stories of brave male missionaries who left their wives and children to do "great exploits" for God. These stories often have a flip side, including the resentment of children who did not know their father. It is not uncommon that when missionary children, or those from ministerial families, gather in groups they swap stories of how they were left to fend for themselves in terms of their faith journey. These sad stories are hinted at in Rob Parsons' little book, *The Sixty Minute Father*.

As a church minister, I made an oath not to fail in this particular respect, and I made a covenant to spend regular time with each child as he grew up. However, this did not stop a few of my friends suggesting to me that I was letting my children down when we moved into a rough inner-city parish as the boys began to go to school. One even said to me, "Your conviction that God wants you to serve the poor is overriding your duty as a parent." I was unimpressed and ignored what I took to be an overly invasive comment, but I sometimes wonder if this early choice of parish was detrimental to my children's education. Is it the motivation of the parent that God is looking for, or is it the final outcome with the child's well-being?

Whatever the case, there are several adventures that took place as a result of us heading to the inner city that suggest my parenting was far from perfect. In fact, it often evidenced a somewhat gung-ho attitude to the safety of young boys, and I wonder if they are the nightmares that stick in their heads rather than the glory of adventure.

Caught out on Kinder Scout
(Edale High Peak)

One of the great things about living in the East Midlands is the proximity of the Peak District, and as I knuckled down to a busy ministry in the city of Nottingham, I could feel the call of the High Peaks and the Dove Valley just thirty miles away in Derbyshire. As a result I became acquainted with the Ordnance Survey maps of the area and began planning routes for walking on days off. Keen to get the young family involved, I'd spread the map on the floor at night and we'd discuss the various merits of different routes, thinking about the length of the walk, the amount of climbing, and the proximity to a pub. What I never seemed to think about was the weather forecast, or the necessary equipment to handle it if things got rough. Of course, this was to return and haunt me.

One day we planned a trip to cross Kinder Scout in the Dark Peak. This is a high point in the Peak District, a tall hill often surrounded by mist and looking distinctly like Mordor (in *The Lord of the Rings*) or some other remote and forbidden place to visit. It is not that this moorland plateau is unknown, because it is a National Nature Reserve that looms over Edale at the beginning of the Pennine Way, and it rises more than 2,000 feet to give views as far away as Manchester and even Snowdonia, but walkers talk about it with some reverence. Down in the pub at Edale, you can overhear walkers discussing their route up Kinder Scout and their experiences in the different weather conditions and unusual terrain found at the top.

For us, Kinder Scout became a symbol of the unexplored, the undiscovered region that only the hardy could subdue.

Personally I felt I was fairly experienced in knowing my way around the High Peak, in that I had previously been part of a cross-country run that went over Kinder Scout, and on another occasion I had breezed over the hill, unaccompanied, on a day off from work and found the weather to be beautiful at the top, giving me views in all directions. It was on one such glorious day that I had walked past Kinder Downfall, a waterfall of supreme wonder, and then continued down to The Snake Pass Inn in Dovedale.

It was not long before three small boys and I began to plan the Kinder Scout trip. We all packed a rucksack with a sleeping bag, "just in case we get caught in a blizzard". My rhetoric was to build up the adventure, to make it into a grand journey that only "true explorers" might be able to achieve. I thought I was making the trip scarier than it was. As an after-thought I threw a tarpaulin and a bottle of water into my rucksack, but no food, as we believed we would get a slap-up meal at The Snake Pass Inn. Nor did we take any first aid, weather-proofing or warm kit, because I felt the walk would keep us warm until we got to the pub. On the way to Edale I told the boys about this ancient hostelry with a snake emblem over the main door, a vital staging post on the turnpike between Glossop and Ashopton so that tired horses could be changed.

And so it was that an eleven-year-old, a nine-year-old, and a five-year-old set out with me at 11 a.m. to one of the most extreme walking places in the UK. I knew the hill was a challenge, but I did not realize how extreme the weather could be. We began by ascending Jacob's Ladder, not taking too much time to listen to the cries of exhaustion from the youngest. At the top, a series of clouds came over, preventing us from seeing back into the valley, and this had the effect of immediately dropping the temperature and making us cold and damp. We pressed on through the rock stacks, and as the mist descended I had to resort to the compass, because the route had become obscured. Then it began to rain. It was icy rain that stung the skin and soaked all clothing. I can still remember beginning to feel a total fool as we crouched beside a rock stack with the tarpaulin over our heads, miles from any place of civilization or comfort, and discovering that my compass was moving in circles (there is a magnetic variation on top of Kinder Scout that can affect how a compass finds its bearing). My promise of a warm pub and a successful trip was looking in doubt.

At this point I could have called the trip off and retreated the few miles back down into Edale, but sadly such wisdom was not available to me. I elected to head directly across the mud valleys found at the top of Kinder Scout. Even thinking about this twenty years on makes my toes curl. The upper plateau on Kinder Scout is only level for a short period; it then gives way to a series of muddy run-offs taking the surface water from the top. The resultant terrain is most unusual, effectively a series of muddy valleys that flow into each other, but none of them flowing in any particular direction. To cross this requires an accurate compass and a lot of stamina and good equipment. The other way is to walk around the edge of the plateau (something that became clear to me subsequently). As it was, I set out taking three small boys across a route that is well nigh impossible to traverse, straight across a bog.

We must have been walking for hours, up one mud valley and then down the next, generally endeavouring to head north. Fortunately the wind and rain passed and a clear night fell, with the Plough confirming that we were actually heading north. At around 10 p.m., we reached the end of the plateau, and five miles away, down the hillside, we could see the Snake Pass and the glow of the inn, where presumably they were serving good food and beer and coke.

However, good sense had at last returned to me. We were going no further. We unfurled the tarpaulin in a small gulley and unrolled the sleeping bags, gratefully getting our damp, cold bodies, fully dressed, into their treasured warmth. No burrow ever felt more welcome.

Then I wrapped the tarpaulin over us all so that we were trapped like flies in a crisp bag. We sipped the water from the water bottle and tried not to glance at The Snake Pass Inn far below in the valley. That night we said our prayers and thanked God that we did not need to sleep like this every night – though in truth this was not so bad. Next time we'd do it differently.

And we did. We returned on many occasions.
I remember the mud banks at the top looking truly alien, as though they were from another planet. I remember a juxtaposition in this story, when my brothers had left home and Dad and I returned to Kinder Scout. Except this time when the storm was howling over our makeshift bivvy while we huddled for a quick coffee, it was Dad who suggested heading back, with me raring to go on. Unfortunately for me, my words have been immortalized into a joke when I said, "Dad, you're not the man you used to be." I think Dad saw this as an insult. (BW)
[Dad's comment: He did.]

I think that on this occasion I got away with my faux pas in that although it could have resulted in pneumonia or some other bad outcome, we survived. The story became one of survival. We triumphed against the odds and, surprisingly, I was not blamed by the boys. In fact, this adventure was a wake-up call: I never again travelled without spare clothes, waterproofs, a bothy bag, food, a torch, and a first-aid kit, and I always ensured we all had hats and gloves. Strangely, in different ways the boys grew up to be very wary of weather conditions and became qualified in mountain rescue. They also reflected on this adventure as a metaphor for the Christian life.

> When I finished my A-Levels at eighteen, I walked the Pennine Way up to Scotland (this begins just before Bleaklow and the Snake Pass). Funnily enough I had learned fairly little from a childhood of having adventures and set off late in the day, in the worst imaginable weather, carrying too much gear and having to camp cold and alone high up on the hill of Kinder Scout. I mention this only to say that it is a memory both vivid and fond. I finished the 280-mile walk (with a little moral support from my dad and brothers at the weekends) and I continue to walk long paths, having recently come home from the Camino in northern Spain and a trek across the Fagaras Ridge in Romania. Sometimes dangerous adventures are the most real. As Chesterton writes, "An adventure is an inconvenience rightly considered; an inconvenience merely an adventure wrongfully considered.[5]" (JW)

---

5 Chesterton, G. K., "On Running After One's Hat" (1908)

Sailing round the south end of Shuna in a vortex

A similar but different story could be told of the day we sailed around Shuna in an Enterprise sailing dingy. The island of Shuna is situated two miles off shore from Arduaine Pier, lying snug between the islands of Luing, Scarba, and Jura. The tidal flow between these islands can become extreme, setting up whirlpools as the tidal variations meet, the most famous being the Corryvreckan Whirlpool. On the sea chart it marks this place, just south of Scarba, as having "dangerous tidal streams".

However, the island of Shuna is moderately well protected from the wilder weather off the west coast of Scotland and, as long as one pays attention to the tide, it offers some safe boating waters. As a young family we went there on holiday when we could afford it, making full use of the coastal surroundings. Initially we would make rafts to paddle around the inner bay at Shuna pier, then over time we branched out further in open canoes or kayaks. On a sunny summer's day we would organize kayak races or create offshore treasure hunts in which we'd gather clues from points we'd established on the salmon farms or on stationary lobster pot buoys or at the sunken wreck. At some point we speculated on what it would be like to sail around the entire island.

So it was that on one fine day, three small boys and I set off north-west from Shuna pier in the Enterprise sailing dingy, heading anti-clockwise round the island. Initially we were beating against the wind, but given a few long sea legs we were soon around the northern point of the island and heading south, running before the wind down Shuna Sound, leaving the island of Luing to starboard. As we reached the southerly tip of Shuna, the wind veered from a northerly to an easterly, meaning we had to tack around the tip of the island. As this happened we hit a change in the tidal flow such that we were now encountering the tide rushing against us. In order to make any headway, we had to get a close-hauled point of sail, which meant I had myself and the small boys aboard all leaning out across the sides of the boat to balance her as we tried to effect the tack. Noticing that I was getting tense, one of the boys said, "Dad, are you OK?" I replied, "I'm fine now, but please don't talk until we have got round that rock. Then you can shout!"

There was a rock sticking out above water level about twenty feet to starboard, against which I was measuring progress, and we were gaining on it by about an inch a minute (it seemed), while the tide seemed set on dragging us towards it and the wind was not favourable. I was genuinely nervous about having no sea space to turn and was anxious not to hit the rock or capsize. I remember thinking that I was glad we all had our life jackets on, and if we were to capsize, the tidal drift would probably take us down to the southern tip of Craignish Point, three miles south on the mainland. The fact that I was thinking like this reveals my inner anxiety, so I nearly jumped out of my skin when I heard my son roar, "We've done it!" He meant that we had just scraped by the first of the underwater rocks and he was dancing a jig of victory as though we were now in the clear.

I thundered, "Shut up!" and threw the boat about, and we whistled by the rock from a different angle, missing all sorts of rocks by inches. Then suddenly we were in the calmer waters of south-east Shuna and away from the fearsome current, able to tack at our leisure. As we sailed on back to the pier, I began to tremble. We had somehow survived against the odds and we were safe. It was then that I began to critique my wisdom. Why had I attempted to sail these waters with such a young crew? The answer was because I wanted to and because I believed it to be safe. Was I equipped to be let out as a father? What if we had capsized in those cross-currents? What if we had hit that rock?

As with many other escapades, this story was one we would tell many times later. Initially there was a lot of teasing given to the son at whom I had bellowed for his premature celebrations. From his point of view, he felt he was justified in dancing a jig in a close-hauled dingy and singing an Indian war cry, because I had told him it would be OK once we had rounded the tip of the island. If I had said so, why was I also not cheering? The explanation that I had miscalculated was one he could not readily accept. He had considered me infallible at that time.

Subsequently, the story was relived to explain how a boat sails when it is going against the wind. It was also a useful story to explain how to handle cross-currents and to reflect on the effects of tide on a small boat. Years later we would return and examine those underwater rocks and see exactly where they were located, for future reference. It even became a story that was used to describe the complexities of a political debate in parliament or in synod. The concept of prevailing tides of ideology concerning, for example, whether women should be admitted to the episcopate was discussed in nautical terms. The ancient traditional views held by conservative evangelicals or Catholics, forbidding women to hold ultimate authority, were discussed as streams of thinking, and the changing winds of popular thought that affected the outcomes in wider church debate were discussed by teenage boys who could not understand church politics.

Interestingly, all three boys were to grow up unafraid of the water, and two of them even took on temporary work crewing ocean-going yachts. They also had the tools to engage with contemporary debate when their mother became a bishop in the Church of England while their grandfather was a staunch member of a conservative evangelical sect. Again it appeared that the nightmare of health and safety was in fact a cloud with a silver lining.

> I remember this vividly and with pride. It was a story I used to tell to fellow sailors when I worked on tall ships and delivering yachts: the time I cheered our Enterprise round a rocky headland and we almost died! As I've said above, adventures (like stories) require a little danger to make the beauty stand out. Having not died in our little boat, I've since sailed big ships and big seas in the Atlantic, Mediterranean, and Baltic. Dad is now preparing his Drascombe Coaster to sail round Britain, and we'll be there to make sure he doesn't sink. (JW)

Stories of adventure that might damage faith

Reflecting on these near disasters has made me see how we as parents are so easily prone to failure because we ourselves are not fully mature, or fully grown up, and because we might allow our enthusiasms or our ambitions to prevail against our inhibitions.

Since it is the case that we who are less than perfect are called upon to raise the next generation, how is it that we survive?

Maybe the near mishaps on Kinder Scout and at the south end of Shuna are metaphors of how our blundering efforts to pass on a functional faith are achieved in spite of ourselves. In the same way that Jephthah's catastrophic story of parental ineptitude somehow managed not to be edited out of the book of Judges, so too God allows our failures to be part of the process of passing on the faith. Maybe the effective transmission of faith from one generation to another is only achieved when the child is able to see that the human parent is only a shadow of the divine parent. In this way God speaks through the failings of the parent, using parental shortcomings as an aid to teaching wisdom.

> **I think the reason faith isn't carried on is because we don't adventure or explore or take risks. Christians must stop being so boring. This needs to be changed. Where's our thirst for life? (BW)**

If this is so, then God has a hand in the parenting process. Parents must collaborate and not resist. Given this logic, the parent who is looking to pass on faith effectively must not try to supplant the role of God. It seems to me that this is exactly what Jephthah did when he made a rash promise to God, not knowing who God was if he believed he had to give God a sacrifice in recompense for a military victory. (Note I have cited the Jephthah story as the text to introduce this chapter section because I deem this account in Holy Writ [Judges 11:30–31] to be a text of terror.) Then, when it became clear that he was going to have to sacrifice his daughter, Jephthah was so beguiled by his own ego and his own sense of honour that he did not even consider the possibility of retracting his promise and saying that he had made a mistake. Therefore, Jephthah is known in the Bible as the warrior judge who sacrificed his daughter. Surely this is one of the great texts of terror to have been allowed to remain within Scripture, a tragic story of abusive parenting that sits there as an enigma – an embarrassment to faithful nurture.

Maybe there are times in our own parenting story when we do the same thing as Jephthah. We refuse to consider that we have made a mistake. We blindly persist in continuing to act in a way that we previously considered to be correct. We hold on to an outmoded view of God and thereby justify a form of "honour killing" that is neither honourable nor worthy of any legitimate sacrifice. This is what happens when parents cease to be humble, and effectively supplant themselves as God within their children's world. If parents are never honest about the way they fail, nor contrite when they have been inadequate, then the children suffer.

Conversely, it is when parents acknowledge weakness that God might be seen shining through their brokenness.

I wrote a prayer that I hope is honest:

Dear God,
May all that I do mean Love and Honour.
And when I fail,
Allow my brokenness to reflect your sacrifice.

(JW)

For discussion

- How do you relate to working with failure as an essential tool?
- Do you have "virtual health and safety disasters" that have become part of the fabric of your narrative?
- In what ways can you see God working through failure (in the biblical story or in your own life)?

CHAPTER 3

Praying

(A) When We Prayed

The prayer of a righteous person is powerful and effective. Elijah was a human being, even as we are. He prayed earnestly that it would not rain, and it did not rain on the land for three and a half years. Again he prayed, and the heavens gave rain, and the earth produced its crops.

(James 5:16–18)

Prayer has not often had a good press. It is generally derided by those who do not have faith and it is romanticized by those who do have faith. Christian adults tend to hold the idea of prayer in unerring high esteem, but few will practise it with any consistent pattern. If someone does carve out a ritual of prayer, there will often be some who suspect them of legalism. Children frequently see the value in prayer, but will be teased by their friends if they become too serious about it.

Prayer is often seen as a religious activity that involves withdrawing from the real world but is in fact the very pattern of living before the face of God. Prayer is the result of being in habitual relationship with our Father God – a practice that can become like breathing, a consciousness that we are loved and are living as we were created to live.

In his book entitled *Markings*, Dag Hammarskjöld wrote poetically about prayer as a means of being constantly radiated by God in order to live; a process that brings daily renewal. He wrote, "God does not die on the day when we cease to believe in a personal deity, but we die on the day when our lives cease to be illumined by the steady radiance, renewed daily, of a wonder, the source of which is beyond all reason."

It has always seemed to me that children understand this more easily than adults do. It is entirely natural for children to want to involve God in the whole of their lives. Although God might particularly "hang out" at church, they know that God is everywhere. Children who pray expect to encounter God at home, at the breakfast table, in the bathroom, in bed or under the bed, at school, or in the car. This "God–awareness" might provoke a formal prayer, but most likely it will result in informal prayer.

I will now discuss these, along with ritualized prayer, as different forms of prayer that can be encouraged by parents.

Formal prayers

If we are to spend our lives "living before the face of God", there need to be some moments in which we consciously address God, not merely to remember his presence and then get back to forgetting him, but as a means of training ourselves to be constantly aware of him.

Interestingly, it is Muslims who are most adept at this way of praying, in that they pray five times a day, getting up in the night to pray (during the summer months) and bookending their days to include prayers as key fixtures. They learned this practice from the early Christians in the Middle East, who in turn learned it from Judaism.

The nearest I got to teaching regular prayer to three young boys as they grew up was to pray at mealtimes (before we ate), at bedtime, and when we were out on a walk. Mealtime needed to be a brief prayer, because we were hungry and hot food might go cold. Night times or walk times could be more leisurely.

Prayers before a meal tended to be a pause before we started, but it was a good pause: one signalling that we were all gathered in one place and were ready to start. First came the prayer and then the eating. The prayer might be as simple as "Father God, we thank you for this food. Amen", or it might involve thanks for the cook, the people gathered round the table or the day's events, but it was always thankful and it was always short. Interestingly, this habit became so ingrained (almost Pavlovian) that it was almost impossible to start without prayer, including when we had guests, even if those guests did not have a faith in God. I therefore noticed that the ingrained habit prevented embarrassment in mentioning God and it was always taken as being a family ritual by guests, who included some well-versed atheists or humanists. In fact, as the children grew older, these prayers were shared out and could be said by any one of us.

> I remember going to other people's houses where they had a habit of singing their prayer before their meal and I would cringe. I felt that they were trivializing it. I liked

how in our family it was just simple. We would pray
vaguely or with detail, but we didn't waffle. I loved the
compline that we did and the silence it brought. Now I
think that the way we pray with children needs to teach
them how to be quiet. (BW)

Prayers at night were said after the story had been read and
discussed. I know that many families say their prayers when
children are safely tucked up in bed, but we always said prayers
downstairs by the fire, in the low-lit room. I have been taught
various mantras for prayer, but in normal time have kept to a
simple pattern of "thank you" and "please" prayers. The deal is
that we initially stop and look back over the day and offer thanks
for what we have noticed and appreciated ("thank you" prayers),
and then we ask for help in areas where we sense the need for
God ("please" prayers).

So a six-year-old's "thank you" and "please" prayers might be:

> *Dear God,*
> *Thank you for helping me play football this afternoon*
> *and not getting too cross when I was pushed. Thank*
> *you for my teacher, who was nice today, and for the*
> *great chocolate sponge at school dinner.*
> *Please help me not to get grumpy with James. Look*
> *after the Syrian refugees who are cold in their tents*
> *tonight. Help us to find a way to look after them.*
> *Amen.*

Other formulas for prayer that I have encountered are TCP, TSP
and ACTS. TCP is:

- Thanksgiving;
- Confession;
- Petition.

TSP is a different rendition of the above, and similar to the one we used:

- Thank you;
- Sorry;
- Please.

ACTS is a slightly longer version:

- Acknowledgment (of God's person, a time to praise);
- Confession;
- Thanksgiving;
- Supplication.

I am sure that there is no one pattern of prayer to fit all people all the time, but it is useful to consider the various types of prayer possible. In my natural voice I tended to prioritize being thankful or asking over praising or confessing, and I would imagine that different prayer styles will be known by different families.

Looking back, I note that from time to time we would experiment with different patterns or learn certain prayers by heart (see "Ritualized prayer" below), but by and large we adopted the pattern of "please" and "thank you".

> **Do you want to hear a joke? One little boy prays to the Lord, "Dear Jesus, please give me a bike," but his older**

brother laughs and says, "No, you idiot, that's not how
you do it. What you've got to do is steal the
bike and then tell God you're sorry." (JW)

Informal prayers

These are the prayers that spill out as a result of habitual God consciousness and might occur at any moment, or even remain as a lived encounter without words. They might be the quick arrow prayers that are said as we talk to someone ("Please help me to stay calm") or as we meet someone again ("Lord, I forget their name..."). When we encounter informal prayer with children they can say things that make us smile.

I once heard a child say, "I like looking at the clouds, 'cause God draws funny faces in them for me." On another occasion, when I was holding a prayer time with children in a school, one child asked me, "Is it OK if I tell God a joke as my prayer?" Of course I said it was fine, and I recall thinking long about the implied intimacy in that query.

One way of encouraging informal prayer is through active prayers. Active prayers are those that use the body to express prayer and as such they are of particular value when relating to lively young people. The Scriptures are full of prayers that reveal a wide variety of posture in order to externalize inner prayer or worship. For example, the Psalms detail clapping (47:1), kneeling (95:6), and dancing (149:3); 1 Timothy details the lifting of hands in prayer (2:8); and Revelation shows believers lying prostrate before God (4:10).

As a result it seems entirely natural to use the whole of the body to pray. When our children were small we once climbed past the snow line above Bala in Wales, and at midday, when we stopped for lunch, we fell on our backs to make snow angels. Then we lay in our snow angel, looking up at the sky, blowing "smoke" from our mouths and saying "angel" prayers. I remember one angel prayer going something like:

Dear God,
Thank you for this high mountain and all the valleys
and clouds down below. Thank you that we are
warm and happy on top of the world making snow
angels. Please watch over those people down in the
valley. Please send your angels to protect the world
and to bring love and peace everywhere. Help us to
remember that your angels are everywhere doing
your will.
Amen.

If you can pray making snow angels, you can pray anywhere. As the years went by, we prayed while walking and running, jumping, sailing, and kayaking. Personally this has hugely influenced how I pray. The children taught me to be informal with God when I was in a position of intimacy (and not leading public prayers). For many years, while my routine was to go jogging every day, I would devote different sections of the run to particular forms of prayer. The initial warm-up run was a prayer of praise. The uphill sections were devoted to battling out my intercessions and the downhill sections were spent thanking God. Even now as I go sailing I often pray something like:

Lord Jesus,
May the power of your risen life fill the sails of my life.
May I learn to look out for where the wind of your
Spirit is blowing so that I am powered by your breath.
Help me to go where you go and do the things you do,
so that I will carry out your holy and true commands.
Amen.

When I have shared these experiences with other Christians I have found out that families develop different styles of informal prayers. One family I used to visit had developed the habit of the children jumping up and down on the bed as they said their prayers.

Ritualized prayers (ones we learned by heart)

Prayers that have been written down and can be learned by rote have a surprisingly wide range of use in a family context. Initially I believed that such prayers were likely to create empty religious practice that was thoughtless and formulaic. In reality I discovered that ancient prayers often embody a distilled theology that causes deeper reflection. Saying a known prayer in the company of others also has a bonding effect in that we are praying communally and with joint intent. It also signals the fact that there is an order and structure to prayer. Prayers will not go on interminably; they will have an end. In the way we used them, ritualized prayers were often announcing that the time of prayer was coming to an end.

The prayer we learned first was the Lord's Prayer in its modern form, and this would be said after each child had had the opportunity to say his own prayers. In effect it was the last act of prayer, bringing all our prayers together to say:

Our Father in heaven,
Hallowed be your name,
Your kingdom come,
Your will be done,
On earth as in heaven.
Give us today our daily bread.
Forgive us our sins
As we forgive those who sin against us.
Lead us not into temptation
But deliver us from evil.
For the kingdom, the power
And the glory are yours
Now and for ever.
Amen.

This prayer is rich in meaning and history. Jesus taught it as an example of praying that is simple and to the point. Each line has a depth of reflection contained within it. It moves from praise to intercession, from confession to worship. From time to time we would stop and discuss the prayer, breaking it into its component parts in order to pray more carefully.

Another great favourite was the evening collect that could be said or sung, heralding that it was now time to pray:

Lighten our darkness, Lord, we pray,
And in your mercy defend us
From all perils and dangers of this night

For the love of your only Son,
Our Saviour Jesus Christ.
Amen.

This prayer was often followed by the ritual throwing of our compline books at Dad's head, thus signifying the end of our night service. (JW)

However, the all-time great prayer that constantly captivated our hearts was one attributed to St Francis of Assissi. This prayer (the Absorbeat) was:

May the power of your love, Lord Christ,
Fiery and sweet as honey,
So absorb our hearts
As to withdraw them from all that is under heaven.
Grant that we may be ready
To die for love of your love,
As you died for love of our love.
Amen.

I always think that this prayer was valued by the boys because of its mystery. Quite what it means is uncertain, though the medieval sentiments and passions are abundantly clear. The allusions to fire and honey and love are rich and satisfying. The prayer has been written by a person with deep feelings for God and it can be said from the heart.

When we learned to say the Absorbeat, I had started going to Franciscan friaries for my annual retreat, and I used to tell the boys how the friars prayed. We began to incorporate saying psalms together at the time of our evening prayers. We found huge delight in saying the psalms responsively or antiphonally and by pausing at the half-line, "just like the friars do". In due course this was to graduate into saying compline at night. Compline is the last prayer of the day said by friars before going to bed. I purchased small compline books and these would be handed out after the evening story. Once we all had a booklet, we would distribute the prayer tasks. One person would lead it, another would select the psalm and detail how it was to be said, another would select the Bible reading, and yet another would lead the intercessions. Initially I would lead the compline service until we were all familiar with the essential pattern, and then I shared the tasks out. As the boys reached secondary school age, they became the leaders of compline. They always saw it as a privilege.

As the years went by, the boys made their own journeys to the friary and enjoyed their own retreats. Now I notice that compline is a regular part of their adult ritual and certainly an expected feature at any homecoming.

At university I used to go to compline and benediction at Magdalen College each week. This was a late-night service, held by candlelight, very simple and very beautiful. I highly commend the pattern of the old monastic services for those who find standard Sunday church services bland. There is much to be said for the balance and flow of a day that moves between matins, vespers and compline (morning, evening, and night prayer), as I learned from living with the Franciscans at Hilfield Friary. (JW)

For discussion

- Do you relate to creating a prayer formula (e.g. TCP, TSP, or ACTS) when teaching prayer patterns to children?
- What do you think about teaching prayers that are memorized?
- When should formal prayer (or informal prayer) be used with children?

(B) When We Found God to Be Absent

But I cry to you for help, LORD;
in the morning my prayer comes before you.
Why, LORD, do you reject me
and hide your face from me?
From my youth I have suffered and been close to death;
I have borne your terrors and am in despair.
Your wrath has swept over me;
your terrors have destroyed me.
All day long they surround me like a flood;
they have completely engulfed me.
You have taken from me friend and neighbour –
darkness is my closest friend.

(Psalm 88:13–18)

A key part of the Christian life appears to be the art of learning to carry on when God does not seem to be there. This, of course, is an aspect of mortality as we discover our own frailty and realize that in some ways we are alone on the journey of life. Our faith that God is there can diminish to a faint flicker and even appear to have gone out. The question then is what we do with our habits of prayer. Do we stop praying in order to be true to our feelings, or do we push on and run the danger of superficiality or hypocrisy? As parents, should we share our doubts and fears with our family, or should we keep them to ourselves?

This is the best example of that wheat and chaff point. You can tell a good story that points to truth, or you can tell a lie. You can have an adventure that teaches you something, or you can do something stupid and dangerous. You can talk about philosophy with the will to seek God, or you can grandstand and make an idol of your own intellect. Your relationship to church can be healthy or damaging. Obviously none of the above are really either/or. I'm well aware that you can learn a great deal after doing something stupid and dangerous. But I'm not sure you can ever pray badly. Even the worst, least meant, most vindictive cry to God is a desire to talk to him who is compassion, love, justice, and mercy. And you cannot go wrong if that is who you are talking to. What Dad and Mum taught me is that what matters is that you pray; you keep trying to make contact. How can you build any relationship without communication?

Also, if it is a real relationship, then the tone of the conversation will change. Sometimes it will be formal, sometimes extremely casual, sometimes intimate, sometimes challenging and defiant. Just as in any human relationship, the sign of healthy prayer is getting past politeness and into honesty. Politeness is not bad, but it serves as the soothing introductive balm to real relationship and nothing more.

Perhaps the most powerful thing I have taken from both Mum and Dad on prayer is the honesty thing. I never felt that any attempt was made at concealment in our storytelling or adventures. When Dad was unsure of something, be that a theological point or whether we would make it round Shuna point, I could always tell. That wasn't because I was especially perceptive, but merely because he never attempted to hide it.

And this became implicit in our learning about talking to God. If he was who we thought him to be, then not only was anything but honesty pointless, but also it meant you could have the freest of all possible relationships with him. Nothing was off the table, nothing was unseemly or grubby, nothing (or rather perhaps everything) was sacred and worthy of being brought to God. Enough said really. (NW)

Allowing for lament in our parenting

In Psalm 88, the psalmist is quite frank about feeling that God has rejected him and turned against him. He feels alone and deeply depressed. He then communicates this publicly by way of lament, writing a psalm that was to be said in the place of corporate prayer.

There are many other passages in the Bible where the prophets or priests or leaders showed a similar uncertainty in their trust in God. As I have considered this inevitable cycle of doubt and faith, I have always been drawn to that statement offered by Habakkuk at a time when his heart was pounding and his lips were quivering, expecting his nation to be invaded by a foreign enemy. At that moment he wrote these memorable words:

> *Though the fig tree does not bud*
> *and there are no grapes on the vines,*
> *though the olive crop fails*
> *and the fields produce no food,*
> *though there are no sheep in the sheepfold*
> *and no cattle in the stalls,*
> *yet I will rejoice in the LORD,*
> *I will be joyful in God my Saviour.*
> *The Sovereign LORD is my strength;*
> *he makes my feet like the feet of a deer,*
> *he enables me to tread on the heights.*
>
> **(Habakkuk 3:17–19)**

This has become the quintessential text of the Worsleys, marking as it does my dad's favourite book of the Bible and reflecting something of both the writer's worldly cynicism and transcendent poetry. It was read with pride at my wedding last year. (JW)

Habakkuk's writings reveal a deep realism to the terror of life and the lack of positive outcomes that might accompany the life of faith, and in the midst of this he states that he will make the choice to opt for faith. He will make belief in a benevolent God his default position. Even if the crops of figs, grapes, and olives fail and the livestock of sheep and cattle do not reproduce, he will learn to be joyful. In many ways this was something I tried to make my default mode as a parent; namely to state my doubts (if I was not sure of where God was in a given situation), but to equally say that I expected God would make things clear sometime in the future.

To go further, when sadness comes calling, when the shadow of death touches the child's world, I believe that it must be addressed with lament. Whether that sadness is confronted "face on" or obliquely is always an area of debate. Many parents think it improper for a child to attend a funeral because it might upset them, but I query the wisdom in this.

When I was a vicar in my mid-thirties and my sons were at primary school, they got to know a girl at the church whom they valued as a friend. She was slightly older than them and was the leader of their youth section, but she was a troubled child, often affected by depression and with strong mood swings. Directly after finishing her GCSEs, she left home and acquired an apartment in a nearby block of high-rise flats. A few weeks after moving into the flat she was upset by another resident, and in a rush of emotion flung herself from the top of the tower block and died. For weeks after, and indeed ever since, my sons were deeply affected by this event and it has been something they have often reflected on. They were insistent on attending the funeral, mourning and saying their bit.

At times, any words seem deeply inadequate. Any attempt to offer comfort by appealing to faith appears trite. The poet Tennyson, writing about the death of his friend Arthur Hallam, expressed his grief with deep poignancy in his epic poem "In Memoriam":

Be near me when my light is low,
When the blood creeps, and the nerves prick
And tingle; and the heart is sick,
And all the wheels of Being slow.

Be near me when the sensuous frame
Is racked with pangs that conquer trust;
And Time, a maniac scattering dust,
And Life, a Fury slinging flame.

Be near me when my faith is dry,
And men the flies of latter spring,
That lay their eggs, and sting and sing
And weave their petty cells and die.

Be near me when I fade away,
To point the term of human strife,
And on the low dark verge of life
The twilight of eternal day.

"In Memoriam", Canto 50, Lord Tennyson

Writing as if praying, Tennyson shows the depths of his suffering over the loss of his loved one, and by articulating this grief, there is a sense that it is better expressed than left inside. The art of true parenting is to be real, and one of the key aspects of reality is to teach that uncertainty is often with us and doubt is a companion to faith.

Clearly, careful consideration needs to be given to how it is taught when a child is growing up, and the appropriateness of exposing the child to darkness needs to be reflected upon. I have settled to a perspective that says that to withhold doubt from one's family (including the children) is likely to be destructive, and ultimately shows a lack of trust in the other. However, I equally resist the notion that children should be used for a parent's therapy and have to listen to the unprocessed rants of the conflicted adult. What is called for is a mediated offering of reflected pain that is increased as the child grows older. In other words, the believing parent can hint at their own lack of faith as well as their own acceptance of faith. They need to mix the dark threads with the light threads in revealing the pattern of life.

This perspective is held by many educationalists and psychologists who discuss the progress of the healthy child. Erik Erikson (1950) is helpful in outlining that, as a human being develops, there is a foundational period in life in which the child learns both trust and mistrust. It is essential for a child to be loved and to experience trust in a safe environment, but if a child encounters *only* trust, then discernment and competitive instinct are less likely to accompany their growth.

Teaching a child to accept loss

The question remains as to how a parent should open up their child to encountering the pain of life. How might a Christian parent make room for the complexity or uncertainty that accompanies faith? How do children experience loss without being destroyed as they grow up? Clearly it is essential that every child begins to understand mortality and to discover where they fit into life, but how are the appropriate limitations to be taught? How is fear of the unknown to be taught without the child becoming anxious?

This is where some of the great educationalists come to our aid. Vygotsky, writing on thought and language in 1962, described the need for the nurturing adult to tell stories to their children that allowed them to experience the darkness from a safe place. Sitting on a parent's knee, the child can address the hobgoblins and ghouls of the dark forest and thereby begin to engage with the terrors of the subconscious and the future unknowns of life. He called this safe place of encounter "the zone of proximal development". Working with this concept, Bettelheim (1976) made a study of the dark meaning of fairy stories and suggested that fairy stories, such as Hansel and Gretel (who are led into a lonely wood and entrapped by a wicked witch), do not actually traumatize a child because they are narrated within the zone of proximal development. The parent first creates a comfortable world in which the child is tucked up in bed, on the shoulders of Dad, snuggling into a lap, around the table, or sitting on the sofa at storytime, and it is in these places that the unknown outside world can be viewed through the lens of story. Bettelheim suggests that it is in this place of safety where children should hear stories that are painful. It is here that they can encounter complexity or even stories that lack resolution. And it is in this place that the child will develop. The stories of loss become vital for growing children as they encounter the difficulties of life.

In my wider writings (Worsley 2009) I have studied how children respond to harsh stories in the Bible, like "Jephthah's Return" (Judges 11:29–40) or "Abraham and Isaac on the hill" (Genesis 22:1–19), stories I call "texts of terror", and I suggest that they can become conversation starters with children that open up a reflected theology in the child if the adult storyteller allows for reflection.

As I write these thoughts I am aware that there are many parents who will deeply disagree with the need to expose children to pain, and who will believe that it is always right to protect the child from all darkness for as long as is possible. My contention is that we as parents cannot live the lives of our children. They have to learn how to discern between good and evil. They must find tools that equip them to make sense of loss and they must learn how to lament. This allows them to be formed for faith.

> Once, Dad let us join him when a friend asked him to help out in slaughtering his pigs. He had not wanted to kill these pigs, but local children were throwing bottles into their pen, and the pigs were chewing them, and the glass was ripping their insides up. We were present as the man from the abattoir slit their throats. I remember watching one pig, laying on its side in a pool of blood, running, as if to some imaginary place. When I've told people about this, they've often recoiled in horror that a child was exposed to such a thing. But I was never horrified. I think it gave me better respect for the animals I eat. Dad allowed us to prepare the meat after the pigs had been killed. (BW)

On a dark night, however, I sometimes wonder if such exposure to "reality" has been of value in the process of parenting. We are all called upon to enter "the dark night of the soul" at times, but we cannot plan it for our children.

The dark night of the soul

It was St John of the Cross who first used the concept of "the dark night of the soul" as being the journey of the soul through trouble and adversity in a search for God. It is a poem written with passion and deep yearning, similar to the poetry of the Song of Songs.

> *Upon my flowery breast,*
> *Kept wholly for himself alone,*
> *There he stayed sleeping,*
> *And I caressed him,*
> *And the fanning of the cedars made a breeze.*
>
> *The breeze blew from the turret as I parted his locks;*
> *With his gentle hand He wounded my neck*
> *And caused all my senses to be suspended.*
>
> *I remained, lost in oblivion;*
> *My face I reclined on the Beloved.*
> *All ceased and I abandoned myself,*
> *Leaving my cares forgotten among the lilies.*
> **"Songs of the Soul", St John of the Cross**

St John of the Cross's notion of being wounded for love has caught the imagination of poets and scholars, many of whom link it with the story of Jacob wrestling with God through the night until he is finally wounded in his hip joint (Genesis 32:24–26). The dark night brings a woundedness that is caused as the spiritual journey of the ego breaks down and the illusions of life give way to a deeper reality. This experience is likely to become familiar to parents raising their children within the Christian faith, watching them grow up, develop independence, and then move away. It often feels like alienation or spiritual depression, or a sense of confusion or disorientation. However, it is a mark of development as a new openness to God and a new maturity is discovered.

For discussion

- Reflect on how loss or failure or disappointment is taught to children. Do you agree with the belief that lament is a crucial aspect of development?
- What difficult (dark?) stories have you shared with children that have brought about effective learning? Why was this?

CHAPTER 4

Philosophizing

(A) When We Philosophized

We do not use deception, nor do we distort the word of God. On the contrary, by setting forth the truth plainly we commend ourselves to everyone's conscience in the sight of God.

(2 Corinthians 4:2)

Back in 1977 Edward Robinson wrote a wonderful book entitled *The Original Vision: A Study of the Religious Experience of Childhood.* These insights, published by the Oxford Religious Experience Research Centre, were to inspire a host of key researchers, including John Westerhoff, David Hay, and Jerome Berryman, who went on to pay close attention to what children were saying about their spiritual experiences. To me the book was wonderful because of its simplicity. It was simply a record of adults remembering childhood experiences and a way of valuing those half-remembered and half-forgotten influences that shaped their lives.

The research was not complex – it was as straightforward as asking people to recall spiritual experience without judging it, categorizing it, or interpreting it. Partly influenced by this and by the writings of Alister Hardy and then John Hull, I began to interview adults who similarly had access to childhood spiritual experiences. This was to lead to me researching a PhD entitled "The Inner Child as a Resource to Adult Faith Development", which I completed in 2000.

Those years of listening to adults who were recycling their childhood experiences and discovering faith allowed me to become more certain of what I had always presumed, namely that faith discovered in childhood can be a resource throughout life. From the samples of adults who talked to me, the common theme to the survival of a lifelong Christian faith was that they had been given permission to explore their faith. Functional faith stemming from childhood had been grounded when it was discussed in a safe environment, when the children had been able to explore it imaginatively and critically in order to make sense of it.

As a result of this, I consciously made space for faith discussions with my own children – conversations that were not manipulated by my constructs and were allowed for wider reflection. These conversations might be called "philosophizing".

As you may have noticed, I find it difficult to talk about the subjects in this book as separate entities. Some of this is because my experience of growing up had it all mixed together: stories, adventures, praying, philosophizing, and doing church all blended into one another. However, I also think that the other reason I find making distinctions tough is because of the habit of philosophizing.

To my mind, doing philosophy is about noticing how things are connected. And the more you do it, the more you realize that ALL things are connected, which if you believe in God isn't really all that surprising.

This habit has had a huge effect on my identity and outlook as I have become an adult. At its best, this habit of philosophizing has helped me to reconcile things that at first seem totally disparate; to find the connections between a God who loves us and the suicide of a friend. Or to understand what connects people who have a deep faith in God but huge differences of opinion on things such as homosexuality and other faiths. Our discussions on God and the world have helped me to form my own ideas too and develop a flexibility of thought that has allowed me to live and work alongside people with whom I have often deeply disagreed. (NW)

Recalling philosophical moments when faith was questioned

A key moment in my own childhood, when I felt I had discovered a way in which the Bible was in contradiction with itself, occurred when I was about ten years old. I had been informed that Scripture could never fail to harmonize with itself, even if it looked to be doing so. I had been to church on a Sunday and heard a sermon that was about God being light and dwelling in light. The text was: "This is the message we have heard from him and declare to you: God is light; in him there is no darkness at all" (1 John 1:5).

However, I had recalled a passage from the book of Isaiah that said something like God created light and darkness. I got a chair and climbed up to pull out a heavy Bible concordance, and was both pleased and disconcerted to discover the verse: "I form the light and create darkness, I bring prosperity and create disaster; I, the Lord, do all these things"(Isaiah 45:7).

I was perplexed, and I carefully stored this thought in my head and reasoned that there had to be a logical explanation. How could God create darkness and light and then say that he only inhabits light? I wondered if I had discovered something that my dad had never thought about.

I finally plucked up courage to talk about it and I was quite surprised to find that my dad was not perturbed. At first he was unsure if I had got my Old Testament reference right, but when I showed it to him he said something like, "God is beyond comprehension." Looking back on this response from my father, I was delighted that he had been so open to ambiguity or mystery in his theology.

I soon worked out that my father showed the same philosophical openness to some aspects of doctrine, though on some issues he could be remarkably fixed. I therefore attempted to encourage philosophical conversations with the boys in order to allow our discourse to remain open to wonder and exploration, as far as was possible. For example, I recall being pleased when one of them asked if it was possible to see the face of God, and on that occasion I had sufficient confidence to turn the question back so that we all had a great family conversation. The youngest members of the family thought it obvious that you could see God, because God walked with Adam in the Garden of Eden and because God became one of us by becoming human in Jesus. The older members of the family said that this was only part of the truth, because in the Old Testament it says that you cannot see God and live (Exodus 33:20). We had discovered a paradox, and this caused us endless speculation as to how to understand and interpret Scripture.

The most meaningful conversations were those that appeared dangerous at the time because as a parent I was not able to steer them towards a settled conclusion and because I was out of my depth in what I personally believed. Such a conversation came when we were reading *The Lord of the Rings* by J. R. R. Tolkien.

In this novel, a representative group of honourable people from Middle Earth set out on an adventure to get rid of a "ring of power" that has the toxic ability to corrupt the wearer. The main protagonist in the story is an unlikely hero, a little hobbit named Frodo Baggins, accompanied at all times by his friend Sam Gamgee. Over several books and through the most complex of situations, these hobbits manage to survive against dark powers, hostile enemy troops, a huge spider, betrayal in their own ranks, and finally extremes of thirst and hunger. To make matters worse, they are constantly followed by Gollum, a malicious and dangerous creature who is tormented by his own inner demons and who occasionally manifests as a less toxic version of himself (named Smeagol).

As we read the book over many months, the question emerged as to whether Gollum could ultimately be numbered with the faithful. Could Gollum be redeemed, and cast off his darkness and inner anxieties, by being accepted by Frodo? In fact, could Gollum be saved?

This question was aired one night as we read the story. Of all the dark creatures in the book – trolls and goblins, Balrogs, and "Dark Riders" – it was only Gollum who actually caused fear in the boys, possibly because they identified with a character who was not perfect, or possibly because I played him up and gave him a distinctive voice. However, the overall hope was that he would ultimately emerge as a healed character.

At the end of the story, it becomes clear that Frodo cannot ultimately get rid of the ring. He knows he must throw it into the volcanic fires of Mount Mordor, but he discovers that he has worn it for too long, that the darkness of the ring has finally gained power over him. When all seems lost, Gollum, who has been skulking in the shadows, leaps forward and bites the ring from Frodo's hand, removing his finger along with it, and in his moment of triumph falls backwards with the ring into the volcano.

I will never forget that on reading this one of my sons rushed out of the room and would not come back. He would not discuss it that night. At a later date he explained why he felt this was the wrong way to end the book. Why should Gollum, who had had such a dark and unhappy life, be a tool to help the hobbits (and the whole of Middle Earth) to survive? Surely if this book was true to the gospel, then Gollum would have been saved?

Dad doesn't mention that I was upset to the point of tears at Gollum's death. The sense of injustice I felt at such a pitiable character's death, and the sense of certainty I had in God's ability to reconcile it, has remained vivid in my memory; the bishop being there has not. (NW)

In subsequent months and even years later we returned to this episode, and the discussion became one about salvation. Could the atonement of Christ save everyone? Could Judas be saved? Could the devil be redeemed? The debate over universal salvation had come to our home and it was to continue indefinitely. In many ways I knew that I had no control over this huge theological controversy. This was a subject that few theologians agreed upon in any detail. And the fact that I was so uncomfortable seemed to add fuel to the discussion. Looking back, I now believe that this was one of the best ways of discussing the teaching of the Bible; namely by doing theology with children and allowing complexity to develop without it being suppressed.

> Ignoring the difficult (and also more interesting) questions just pushes the child toward asking them away from the parent. (BW)

Philosophy4Children

I later discovered that philosophy became a significant means by which primary school children were helped to develop their thinking and gain confidence in their own perspective. In the early part of the twenty-first century it actually became patented as P4C (or Philosophy4Children): a model of classroom engagement for learning.

On its website, among the many benefits for children P4C details that it:

- is an enquiry-based approach to open up children's learning through the exploration of ideas;
- gives children the possibility of seeing that their ideas have value, and that others have different ideas that have value too;
- allows children to realize that they don't always have to be right;

- creates the confidence to ask questions and learn through discussion;
- allows all learners (including teachers) to have opportunities to genuinely enquire;
- offers a chance to speak and be heard without fear of getting an answer wrong;
- allows intelligence to grow;
- gives children who are not considered "academic" a voice and a chance to flourish;
- gives the "academic" children a chance to think outside the box and to see that the non-academic have inspiring ideas;
- gives all children value.

I particularly like the second and third objectives from P4C (i.e. giving children the possibility of seeing that their ideas have value, and allowing children to realize that they don't always have to be right).

When we were children Dad read us a book called *The Little Prince* (by Antoine de Saint-Exupéry), which truly illustrated the value of the child's perspective. It made such an impression that I wanted to read this out loud to children, like Dad did to me. Unfortunately, I think my tastes are not shared by the children in the classes that I teach, as *The Little Prince* has flopped. Maybe I didn't introduce it properly, or maybe it's a children's book loved by adults more than children. (In protest I have had the picture of a boa constrictor swallowing an elephant tattooed onto my right arm.) (BW)

When parents make space for faith to be questioned

I did not realize it at the time, but through philosophizing we had stumbled on a jewel in education. It was the means whereby we would engage with many other philosophical texts, including Nietzsche, Camus, and Kierkegaard. In subsequent conversations, if the philosophical text opened up a conversation, we would stick with it. If it became too dense or obtuse (or maybe we did not understand it), we would let it go.

One book that I remember Dad reading to us was *Sophie's World* by Jostein Gaarder (an excellent and entertaining introduction to the world of philosophy, framed by an exciting mystery, well worth reading by anyone). There's a bit in the book about looking at stars and realizing that the light from them has taken many millions of years to reach us and that we may be looking at something that seems to be alive but is in fact now dead. I remember Dad taking us out to the banks of the River Leen, near where we were living in Radford, and getting us to lie on our backs looking up to the stars while he read. Plato said it best: "Philosophy begins in wonder.[6]" (JW)

For discussion

- Do you agree that children are natural philosophers (or natural theologians)?

6 Plato, *Theaetetus*

- When should the parent (or teacher) be alongside the child as enquirer?
- How does an adult enquire alongside the child?

(B) When Our Philosophizing Was as Blowing in the Wind

See to it that no one takes you captive through hollow and deceptive philosophy, which depends on human tradition and the elemental spiritual forces of this world rather than on Christ.

(Colossians 2:8)

I am deeply aware that philosophy needs to come with a Christian "government health warning" and that there are many dangers of breeding a secularist discourse that can hover around the edges of conversations that are ultimately humanist and not open to the insights of faith. If we as parents are not informed by Christian faith, we act as if we are alone on the planet and we operate as if there is no God. In that case we live our lives by relying on our own reason and intellect as human beings rather than by faith. Philosophy might appear to be our only option in educating our children, but it is dangerous if our philosophy is not informed by faith.

As parents who want to nurture children into faith while also teaching a critical perspective, we are called to tread a subtle journey between the rock called Scylla and the whirlpool called Charybdis. The rock is dogmatic and unquestioned faith, and the whirlpool is the endless rumination of philosophy. We are called to walk on a pathway between certainty and doubt that allows our children to see that having faith includes questioning and that being a Christian does not mean bidding farewell to the brain.

For Christian parents, maintaining this balance is an art form. As St Paul wrote to the early church in Colossae, we must be aware of trusting human logic rather than Christ (Colossians 2:8). This is a frequent theme throughout the Hebrew Scriptures and the New Testament; namely that reason is only useful up to the point where we trust God and do not lean on our own understanding (Proverbs 3:5). It is the balance between divine insight and human wisdom.

This was well known by Christian philosophers in the past. The fourth-century saint Augustine coined the phrase that theology is "faith seeking understanding" to describe this tension. This phrase was taken up again and popularized by the philosophical theologian Saint Anselm in the eleventh century. But, so often, we who enjoy playing with academic ideas and constructs can ultimately attempt to achieve divine understanding through cognition rather than revelation. We have to learn that philosophy is not an end in itself. Without the Spirit of Christ, philosophy is the art of blowing in the wind.

Just as in everything else, there is a shadow side. If you can make connections to everything from everything, then it is easy to lose your way. Instead of helping you to understand another person's point of view, or helping you to decide your own thoughts, making all these connections merely serves to muddy the waters. You can come away with a wishy-washy sense that everybody is right, or that it doesn't really matter what you do because it's all just connected anyway. Like. . . totally cool, man.

So, how do you find out if all that philosophizing is doing you good or if it's just an easy way to allow you to think whatever you want? In the same way that storytelling and adventures balance each other out, so too does philosophizing. (NW)

Showing off/looking good

One of the sins of parenthood is to try to appear intelligent to our offspring. This is not only a sin of the theologian who wants to show complexity of thought; it is often the sin of any father or mother who wants to gain approval from their nuclear family. While writing this section of the text I took a break to watch the highlights of the weekend football and noticed two premier football players each saying in their post-match interview that they particularly enjoyed scoring a goal because their small son was watching. One player said, "What father does not want to be a super-hero to his son?"

Dad is not immune to this. We have a joke that he still likes to think he could kill a man with one punch. Sure thing, Dad. (JW)

And so it is with theology. If we indicate that we as parents hold the keys to understanding what is divine, then we are likely to become unstuck. Maybe we can hold an academic viewpoint or even defend an orthodoxy, but have we allowed our faith to be wrestled with in sufficient depth so that God is encountered? Do

127

we allow our children to go through "the dark night of the soul" in reality testing for God?

Recalling philosophical moments when faith was not allowed to be questioned

Like most parents who hold fast to a particular belief, I had moments when I did not want my faith to be challenged by anyone, and certainly not by my children. Of course, in my periods of security, I was open to other insights and willing to allow my children to wrestle with their own beliefs as they engaged with my perceptions, but there were times when I shut down conversations and offered dogmatic or prejudicial viewpoints. I did not want to be challenged and I did not have the mental energy to allow for theology to be reflected upon.

Looking back, I must accept with some candour that I hold strong views and therefore as a parent I have steered conversations away from controversy or towards my own convictions when discussing any issue that I am passionate about, including theological subjects.

I probably did this over issues of human sexuality until such time as the lads had left home as young adults, but I wonder if I did this over other aspects of theological controversy as the boys went through their teenage years. Certainly questions concerning the virgin birth or the divinity of Christ were ones that I would have left to others to debate with my children, and I wonder if this caused them to think that I had no diversity of thought on such topics.

In the wider literature of parenting for faith is the priceless 1907 memoir entitled *Father and Son* by Edmund Gosse. In this moving account, the literary critic details his childhood in the religiously conservative and biblically literalist world of the Plymouth Brethren, a nineteenth-century sect. The Brethren were a breakaway movement from the Church of England endeavouring to show a greater reliance on the historic biblical texts. The Holy Scriptures form a backcloth to the whole book, particularly the struggle of Philip Gosse (the father), an influential invertebrate zoologist and marine biologist who was responding to the new evolutionary theories of his scientific colleague, Charles Darwin.

As the book develops, the story is told of the young Edmund Gosse seeing his learned father squeezing his scientific insights of the fossil world into a literal understanding of the six-day creation described in the early part of Genesis. In the fifth chapter of the memoir, Gosse observes his father, working alongside his main researcher Philip Carpenter, resolving "to have nothing to do with the 'terrible theory' of Darwin's theory of evolution, but to hold steadily to the law of the fixity of species" (p. 103). His father was to write up his own theory, refuting Darwin's work, in a book entitled *Omphalos* in 1907, subtitled "An Attempt to Untie the Geological Knot". Put simply, his understanding was that God had hidden fossils in the rocks at the time of creation, in order to test the faith of later geologists.

Seen through the eyes of an eight-year-old son, this was "a fallacy, if he could have known it, but he [Edmond's father] allowed the turbid volume of superstition to drown out the delicate stream of reason. He took one step in the service of truth, and then he drew back in agony and accepted the servitude of error" (p. 102).

It is clear that this was to be a defining moment for the young Edmund, looking at his father from his innocent perspective.

Publishing his thoughts half a century later in 1857, his memory was that his beloved father was "to bring all the turmoil of scientific speculation to a close, fling geology into the arms of scripture, and make the lion eat grass with the lamb" (p. 105).

Much of this memoir is the reflection of an adult revisiting the repression of literalist thinking on the emergent intelligence of a creative son who loved his religious father. It is clear that the book is written with a certain reluctance, anxious to defend his father's integrity, but insistent on showing the agony of a child's ability to wrestle with complex thinking and colliding world views. It was published nineteen years after his father's death and shows the constant paradox of unresolved memory. For example, in the epilogue, Gosse states that his father was "no fanatical monomaniac".

Perhaps the most seminal recollection is of the growing boy deciding to scientifically test what his father has told him. Having cross-examined his father as to the meaning of "idolatry" and discovered it to mean the worship of anything other than God, Edmund carries out an act of idolatry to see if God will punish him.

> *I determined, however, to test the matter for myself,*
> *and one morning, when both my parents were safely*
> *out of the house, I prepared for the great heresy. I was*
> *in the morning-room on the ground-floor, where,*
> *with much labour, I hoisted a small chair on to the*
> *table close to the window. My heart was now beating*
> *as if it would leap out of my side, but I pursued my*
> *experiment. I knelt down on the carpet in front of the*
> *table and looking up I said my daily prayer in a loud*

> *voice, only substituting the address, "O chair" for the*
> *habitual one (p. 66).*

He then waits to see what will happen, and when nothing does, concludes that God does not care.

This book offers some unique and personal reflections of a child encountering the Bible in a literal manner and being forced to reflect on it secretly, away from the scrutiny of a caring parent who has a fixed interpretation of the text. As a result, the memoir is poignant, fraught with ambiguity, and written with feeling, long after the death of the father, but still reflecting on meaning, specifically on how to understand the ancient Scriptures.

What is clear from the book *Father and Son* is that the young Edmund Gosse was never allowed any diversity of thought in the way he was parented for faith. It was to take Edmund a lifetime of reflection to articulate his own beliefs as being different from those of his father. As a parent, I have always resolved not to make this mistake.

Considering whether the absence of philosophical moments when parenting for faith becomes abusive

It is important to be careful when using the word "abuse" in terms of a child's development in a religious context, but when biblical ideas are used to oppress children, they can have a damaging impact. The provocatively entitled *The Poisonwood Bible* by Barbara Kingsolver (1998) invites the reader to make a connection between the Bible and "poisonwood", a beautiful Floridan tree that flourishes in tropical America and in sandy dunes by salt water. The wood is heavy and hard, but not strong. It has no commercial value and cannot even be used as fuel. Worse still, the sap contains alkaloids that cause serious skin irritation, so the wood cannot be handled.

In *The Poisonwood Bible*, Kingsolver shows that in the hands of missionary-minded Nathan Price, the Scriptures bring pain and produce little that is of value. The story is told by the five women of the Price family, who move in 1959 from Georgia to the village of Kilanga in the Belgian Congo. The voices in the book change between Orleanna, the wife of the missionary, and her four daughters: Rachel, a teenager, Leah and Adah, two very different twins, and the young Ruth May.

As the girls grow up, they tell the story of their father and the effect he has on their lives as he forces his beliefs upon the Congolese villagers and his patient family. It is a story of fascinating complexity that allows insight into the fifteen-year-old Rachel's resentment at finding herself far from the fashion halls of America. The little Ruth May is only five years old and it is she who has to pay the ultimate price for her father's world view. Leah is the able-bodied fourteen-year-old who tries to support her father in what he is doing, but ultimately cannot. Her twin, Adah, has suffered from hemiplegia since birth and she limps along in silent reflection.

Ultimately the story shows Orleanna protecting herself and her children by leaving Nathan and his terrible God. The tale is almost an antithesis to *The Pilgrim's Progress*, showing the folly and damage of biblical faith as opposed to the resource and reward. The Bible in the hands of Nathan Price leads him towards an inexorable certainty, whereby his faith becomes more fixed and less considered as the context in the Congo becomes more challenging. We see Leah reluctantly observing her father's inability to master the language of the villagers from Kilanga, with the result that he says the opposite of what he intends. The biblical meanings of his gospel become obscured by this lack of attention to culture and result in something entirely sinister. Instead of being a resourceful tool with which to build society, the Bible as used by Nathan Price becomes an irritant and is useless to the society into which it is imported.

At its worst, this model of Christian parenting for faith can be deemed to be abusive, because it does not allow the growing child any room for reflection, nor sufficient opportunity to philosophize and think. An extreme version of this idea is presented in the popular atheist text by Richard Dawkins, entitled *The God Delusion* (2007). Dawkins takes this viewpoint to another level when he considers the mere teaching of religion in schools to be an indoctrination process. He suggests that any religious education in the home or in school is a form of mental abuse, because a young child cannot be considered sufficiently developed to have engaged with independent views on the cosmos and humanity's place within it.

This, of course, is far from the point I am making, and is a view that could be levied at any teaching of new insight to a developing child, but I do nonetheless wish to bear in mind the observation. There exists a deep anger and distrust of organized religion among those like Dawkins, and they show their disdain at unreflected parenting for faith. I am deeply mindful that the resourceful and nurturing process of introducing a child to Christian faith is but a hair's breadth away from the damaging indoctrination of a child who does not yet have the cognitive ability to wrestle with the notion of faith.

Dawkins wrote an interesting book called *The Magic of Reality* (illustrated by my favourite artist, Dave McKean), in which he asks whether or not there needs to be faeries at the bottom of the garden for the garden to be magical. I am most definitely with the faeries on this one. At least, I am not so confident that they don't exist that I would take the chance of killing one through my unbelief. ("Oh, the cleverness of me" eh, Peter Pan?) That said, I strongly agree with Dawkins when he writes, "Do not indoctrinate your children. Teach them how to think for themselves, how to evaluate evidence, and how to disagree with you." This goes for all dogmatic beliefs, including his own. (JW)

For discussion

- How do Christian parents navigate between Scylla and Charybdis (where the rock is dogmatic and unquestioned faith, and the whirlpool is the endless rumination of philosophy)?

- Do you find yourself closing down conversation with your children on certain subjects? Why is this?
- What subjects do you avoid discussing with children? (When is this right and when is it not right?)
- Do you have sympathy with either Philip Gosse (in *Father and Son*) or Nathan Price (in *The Poisonwood Bible*), or do your sympathies lie with their children?
- What do you think of Dawkins' allegation that religious education in the home is potentially abusive?

CHAPTER 5

Going to Church

(A) When We Included Church as Part of the Kingdom Dream

Let us consider how we may spur one another on towards love and good deeds, not giving up meeting together, as some are in the habit of doing, but encouraging one another – and all the more as you see the Day approaching.
(Hebrews 10:24–25)

It is part of the deal for any Christian who wants to grow in faith, for anyone who is focused on following Christ, that the journey involves going to church. We need to demonstrate that we are part of the visible community of Christians. We are not alone on the journey of faith but are part of a wider body. Therefore as parents we must help our children to meet with other Christians. We must not travel alone in our family unit by constructing an individual faith or living out our faith without reference to others.

> Church provides an external viewpoint. In fact, your average "local church" of 50 to 100 people provides 50 to 100 different viewpoints. (NW)

> Of these five habits I find the last to be a bit of a problem. From my experience I have known friends who have not benefited from this habit. I myself struggle with going to church, although I do appreciate it. I think the key problem is that it can often become a boring meet-up of unrelatable topics and conversation with unrelatable people. (BW)

It seems that even in the first century, meeting together as church was not easy and was a practice that needed encouraging. This is why the writer of Hebrews exhorted the church not to stop meeting together, as some were in the habit of doing.

However, there are many reasons why church attendance is not an easy option for young families. Many churches do not prioritize catering for children in their services, because of their lack of resources or even vision. Quite often churches are struggling to achieve effective mission because of internal conflict or apathy or tiredness. However, Jesus Christ made it clear that he would be present when two or three people met in his name. Although there is no formula as to what happens when Christians meet, the church that met at the beginning of the Acts of the Apostles "devoted themselves to the apostles' teaching and to fellowship, to the breaking of bread and to prayer" (Acts 2:42).

If a young family is to join in and play a part in this story of the gathered church, then it must have a vision for the church. It must be able to dream of what the church could be like, as well as accept what it is like.

> I think it's important that you don't turn off your critical function when it comes to the church. It always helped me to know that I wasn't alone in thinking that church was boring. Yes, even priests can hate going to church. Let's be honest, church is often dull, and accepting this may be the first step to changing it, or at least challenging something in the way church is done or the way in which we receive it. (JW)

Dreaming of what church could be like

The art of going to church is the art of being a visionary. Rather than looking at the age range present in church, the "coolness factor" of those who attend, the opportunities on offer, or the "what's in it for me?" factor, the Christian nuclear family needs to learn to see church in rather more glorious terms.

As our little family grew up we worked hard to imagine that church *really was* the gathering of God's people. Church really was where Christ Jesus would join us as we learned how to love each other. Church really was where we might meet an angel. In fact, angels were present every time we broke the bread at Communion. As we built our vision of the ideal church in our minds, we began to believe that church was where other people came because they wanted to meet us as their brothers and sisters. In fact, church was where we were wanted, where we were useful, where we were loved. It was our family.

By starting at the visionary end of reality, we found that the boys accepted church attendance as a given. Now, in our case, the boys did not have a lot of choice, in that when they were small I was the church leader, up at the front preaching or leading. Shortly after I was ordained, Ruth became ordained and she was called to serve at a different church during her initial training. Therefore we were challenged to find ways of keeping three primary-school-aged boys engaged while we led the main act of worship in different churches. The answer did not lie so much in getting them supervised as in getting their support. We discovered that if they felt part of the church, they wanted to go to church.

With Dad and Mum church has always been important. But it wasn't the ritual of going to a specific building and saying some specific words that was important. Rather it was the idea of community and family. If the habit of philosophizing loosely encompasses the thinking we do in the confines of our own heads, then church is the community forum, the place where we take that thinking and test it against others' thoughts. This definition of church is much broader than the common one (that of a building in which holy stuff happens), but I like to think that it is closer to the original definition of church: "For where two or three gather in my name, there am I with them" (Matthew 18:20).

This is why the habit of doing church is so important. Church balances out the habit of philosophizing. Having others to challenge your thoughts helps pull you back from the mire of believing everything and nothing.

> And traditional church doesn't just utilize the physical congregation to challenge you, but also the tradition of those who have gone before, the collected thoughts and ideas of generations of people who have wrestled with the same questions we wrestle with today. (NW)

Of course, there are a hundred and one ways in which churches attempt to include children, and those methods vary in success depending on the temperaments of the children, the skill of the children's leaders, and the adaptability of the church. I remember reading many books, including Peter Graystone's *Help! There's a Child in My Church* and Margaret Withers' *Mission-Shaped Children: Moving Towards a Child-Centred Church*, and these had many good ideas, but at the heart of the issue is how we win the battle of vision and see the church as family; this is core to our survival.

Enduring church (accepting that church is not always cool and neither are we)

Having accepted the fact that I needed the boys (as well as myself and my wife) to have a vision of church, the next question became how we handled it when that vision was clearly not living up to our expectations. So often the real church was light years away from the ideal church because the church was not living up to its calling. Therefore we had to work on the notion that it was our task to help the church to be what it was meant to be. If no one was looking after the children who drifted in from the nearby estate, then it was our job to find out how to do so. If some of the older people attending church were too infirm to get up after the service to go for coffee, it was our job to help them by bringing coffee over to them.

Even as I write this, I am aware of how potentially manipulative it must sound, as it implies that I prevailed on my little family to help out at church, to do the things that were within our capabilities as a family. Looking back, in our case we had no other options. And this policy of engagement seemed to work, in that by being useful and thinking of how we could all help out allowed us to focus on mission and not on our own desires.

I was deeply aware, however, that the day could come when the dream became a nightmare, when the vision of church as God's kingdom would appear to be totally unrealistic to growing boys as they became adults. It would not take much reflection for our children to see that the church fell far short of the ideal vision we had.

Somehow, despite my fears, that moment when the boys would finally reject the church never came. As they grew up in the vicarage, our children learned to endure church, to love it as it was, warts and all, and to accept it as a part of our lives. As I have reflected on this, I think this was owing to the fact that we had somehow learned to accept church not for its potential but for what it was. We had all learned to accept that we fitted into a pattern of life that did not question whether you went to church. In simple terms, there was no option, either for the boys or for us as vicars. I also think that it was because we were realistic and honest with them. We discussed the failures of the church as well as our vision for the church.

I think the reason we never stopped going to church while at home is because we respected our parents' faith.

Sometimes I was extremely bored and not interested, but I trusted their opinion on it, and if Dad thought it was a good idea, then it probably was. That makes me sound a bit weak-minded, but I think that I trusted Dad's opinion on it because he was actually quite critical of church (even when he was the vicar) and could see its many faults. I think this honest approach made me understand the benefits and the dangers of having a faith without having the viewpoint of the religious community alongside my world view. (BW)

When it became clear that Sunday school had its limitations, we worked on incorporating a regular "all-age component" into the main services. When most services were required to be eucharistic (involving the sacrament of Holy Communion), we learned how to involve children in the service, as well as at the point of receiving Communion.

Looking back, I am aware that this level of involvement achieved a form of "buy-in" with our boys – an early level of compliance that was hugely beneficial to the smooth running of the family home – and I wonder what would have happened if such involvement had not been given to them.

I am also aware that within their network of friends, church attendance did not remain high unless they also felt committed in some way. In those instances where their friends had an arrangement to help out at children's church or youth church, they were likely to show up. Conversely, where the onus remained on the church to provide a suitable youth and children's programme, and to be interesting, the young people were as likely to drift off at some point, considering the option to be less interesting compared to other choices of activity. Maybe it was because when they were treated as customers, young people felt they could shop elsewhere, but when they were treated as family, they joined in with proceedings with some degree of compliance, as if they had nowhere else to go.

> Enough of my adult self giving you his reflected opinion of church. What of me the child and his experiences of church? I have since realized that Mum and Dad worked hard to make church an extension of our family. This meant that as a child I accepted that this was part of who we were, and the people at our church were just people who were part of our wider family. This linking of our small family with the bigger one of church may sound obvious, but it is essential if you want to engage children and young people with church. Children are always more perceptive than adults realize, and if they are relationally invested in the people at church, then church matters, not because the service matters, or the music, but because it's full of people they care about. (NW)

As I write this I am aware that "being useful" is a major factor in why many Christians do not feel the need to go to church. I currently have an MA student researching for a dissertation that explores why men are under-represented in churches. After exploring the literature and speaking to a large cohort of men, he has come to the conclusion that many men feel their presence at church is irrelevant. Even if they believe in God, they wonder about the point of standing there singing. Why sit and listen to a talk about a text when you could be enacting it? However, if they can help out in practical ways, or in visionary ways that consider how society will be changed for the better, then men might want to get involved. Once they feel useful, maybe men will feel wanted at church. And, of course, this does not simply apply to men. It is also likely to be the way women and indeed older children begin to feel in a society that values action and rewards achievement.

The great exception to needing to be useful at church, or to being an essential part of a small team, was Soul Survivor. Soul Survivor was a brand that made Christianity seem cool. It allowed Christian young people to experience what it was to be mainstream, rather than part of a minority subculture, even if only for a brief window in time.

Soul Survivor

I mention Soul Survivor here, because, although the main summer festival ended in 2019, it was incredibly influential. It sprang from Anglican New Wine ministries in the UK and developed its own brand of contemporary and passionate youth ministry. On their website (accessed in 2019) they wrote:

> We run events because we're passionate about seeing people meet with, and be changed by, Jesus. We've often found that as we focus on God he does incredible things; he meets us where we're at, and we are changed. At our events we always give space for three things: times of sung worship, teaching from the Bible and times of prayer ministry.
>
> We also recognise that being a Christian and following Jesus isn't something we do on our own. We put on

*events to encourage one another in our walk with
God and to develop relationship and community with
each other. For this reason our events often have loads
of space just to hang out with each other and have a
laugh!*

Every summer there were four Soul Survivor events lasting
five days, and new events and ideas were constantly being
envisioned. In 2018 around 25,000 young people were welcomed
at the various events throughout the summer. And there were
many other events, such as weekends away, equipping days and
Saturday celebrations, and occasions to support and encourage
youth leaders.

Among the many Christian youth events that operated over
the UK, Soul Survivor was the one major Christian festival that
seemed to have the widest appeal in engaging with a range of
different types of church and even young people on the fringes
of faith. Although our own children did not become huge fans
of the movement, many of their contemporaries found it to
be what they were looking for. It was a bridge between youth
culture and the church.

The reasons for the success of the Soul Survivor festival were
many, but I will offer five.

*1. It was entirely focused on the tribal group of teenagers (it was
not for adults)*

Teenagers are distinctly tribal. As Fowler's *Stages of Faith* (1981)
clearly details, the third stage considers the teenage years to be a
"conformist" stage, a period when they are more aware of their

own perspectives and deeply in need of affirmation. Indeed ,teenagers are very sensitive to other people's expectations but very insecure as they transition from childhood to adulthood. In this stage of a young person's life, authority is located externally. They tend to hold beliefs and values strongly, but without subjecting them to much critical scrutiny. Fowler calls this "synthetic-conventional", a period of transitional faith that can become arrested if it remains too defended or insufficiently challenged. Soul Survivor created a culture where faith in Jesus was no longer the outsider culture but the dominant one that facilitated early Christian nurture. As such it was hugely beneficial to teenagers who were finding their feet as Christians in a secular age.

2. It was unambiguous about its focus on following Jesus

The leadership of Soul Survivor was always clear that it was about youth discipleship and that this was not something to be compromised. Radical discipleship was the DNA of Soul Survivor, and because of this clear emphasis it became a resource to many other youth ministries.

3. It combined worship with social action

While many youth movements became one sided by being too religious and spiritual or alternatively too focused on sporting or political objectives, Soul Survivor remained balanced. It kept its feet on the ground with programmes of social action while connecting to spiritual realities. From a missional perspective, it kept diversity within itself, blending mark two of mission (nurture and discipleship) with mark three of mission (acts of love and compassion).

4. It was a learning and a changing movement

Soul Survivor took time to reflect on what it was doing well and what it needed to change. As such, it was constantly evolving, looking to bring its distinctive brand of discipleship to other areas in the UK and also to export its message around the world. When it ended in 2019, it was because, although still successful, it felt it had accomplished its purpose. It knew when to stop.

5. It was able to absorb a diverse range of people and could accept critique

In their early teens, our sons accompanied me to Soul Survivor when I was visiting the youth camp with a team of students from the theological college, and their initial reflections on the big celebration meetings were that they were hyped and attempting to manipulate youth response. I noted that when they articulated this within the wider group, their perspective was given a voice. In other words, total conformity was not demanded, and divergent thinking was encouraged. It seems that this security in the structures of the movement, this ability to allow for divergence within an overall conforming culture, is what allowed Soul Survivor to effectively nurture postmodern children in a traditional discipleship.

I do not wish to damn Soul Survivor (which I'm sure has been a blessing to many young people), but to be honest my own limited experience of it has been pretty mixed. My strongest memory of Soul in the City (a Soul Survivor event that admirably tried to funnel the energy and enthusiasm of its community into inner-city projects) is of sitting uncomfortably in a huge worship tent as thousands of teenagers were encouraged to vociferously respond to the Spirit (shouting, crying, singing, etc.). Admittedly this is not a culture that I'm overly familiar with, but I found the experience a little alienating. Certainly, I have not experienced the Holy Spirit in that particular way and to me the overall effect smacked more of crowd mentality than something more genuine. Having said that, I can be cynical and do not wish to demean something that may have meant much more to those who experienced it authentically. (JW)

Changing church culture to encourage young people

Most churches cannot constantly be like a Soul Survivor conference (even though there is a Soul Survivor church in Watford, which was founded by the same people). From a parent's viewpoint, it is highly desirable that church culture moulds to include children and young people. Any church seeking to be true to the mission of God has to adopt a diversity in its age range and culture in order to be a witness to the culture in which it is embedded. If a church focuses on only one culture or age group, it might achieve a limited form of success and prove to have appeal to a particular grouping, but it will be less than it could be.

Missiologists have a term for the principle used by churches that deliberately target only one seam in the strata of humanity: the "homogenous unit principle" (HUP). If a church is to avoid becoming a single homogenous unit (for example, only appealing to the over-sixties or to the young and singles), then it must learn how to change its culture to welcome children and be open to their insights.

Welcoming children in church

Most churches are deeply aware that they would like to see more children in church, but are not sure how to achieve this. In simple terms, they must adopt certain practices and become open to change. The presence of children in the church will change the way a church operates on a Sunday, as well as mid-week, because children are not merely a target grouping but a core group within and through which God is speaking and working.

There are various ways that children can be welcomed in church, and many of them have been highlighted in the recent Church of England report "Rooted in the Church" (2016), the key findings of which I detail further down. Of these I will identify four: Children in Communion, youth confirmation, servers or choristers, and youth group services.

Children in Communion

Admitting children to Communion is key to helping them to be accepted. In Anglican churches the practice over the last century had been to admit children to Communion once they were confirmed, often when they became teenagers, but this practice coincided with the widespread cessation of church attendance after Communion was permitted. Further reflection on this suggested that there was no definitive theological reason not to admit baptized children to Communion from a young age, even before they were cognitively able to understand the sacrament in any robust way. Interestingly, it has always been the practice of orthodox churches to admit infants to Communion from the point of baptism. As a parent I noticed how this simple admission to Communion was a huge benefit to our children growing up, and I can well remember the early struggle to persuade our churches to become part of the early Anglican experimentation in this – a habit that is now widespread.

In churches other than Anglican churches, the encouragement for children to be full members in the breaking of bread is equally to be supported when they express a desire to be involved.

> I remember feeling mortally offended as an eleven-year-old in Catholic primary school when I was not allowed to receive communion at Mass, despite being included in our own church. Distinctions between Christian denominations mean very little to children, and this is probably how it should be for all those who encounter Christ in the other. In other words, if Eucharist means unity, why do we let it divide us? I like this eucharistic prayer written by Donald Reeves, which I first heard used by the Franciscans at Hilfield Friary:
>
> *We break this bread for those who love God,*
> *For those who worship the god of Hindus,*

For those who follow the path of the Buddha,
For our brothers and sisters of Islam,
For the Jewish people from whom we come,
And pray that one day we may become one.

We break this bread for the great green earth,
For the forests, fields and flowers we are destroying,
And pray that one day, God's original blessing will
be restored.

We pray for those who have no bread,
For the hungry, the homeless,
And all who are refugees,
And pray that one day this world may be a
home to all.

We break this bread for the broken parts of ourselves,
For our broken relationships and the wounded child
in each one of us,
And pray that one day we may find the wholeness
that is of Christ.
Amen.

(JW)

Youth confirmation

In Anglican churches the practice of confirmation is normative as a means for young people to articulate that they now accept their infant baptism. It is accompanied by a wider celebration involving other churches and the bishop, thereby signalling that their faith is wider than the church they attend.

As our boys grew up, they were confirmed as teenagers, but this was done in a wider group of other teenagers from across the diocese. In this diocese, teenagers were given the opportunity to meet with a peer group in preparing for their confirmation and then they were given a key role in the service itself. Not only did they choose the music, but they also did the readings and offered public testimony. Those who were too shy to speak in the service itself were videoed beforehand and their testimony played on the big screen. Such attention given to their own culture and sensitivities made the service one that they felt able to ask their friends to attend. It was relatively cringe-free.

> I like the Catholic tradition of taking a new name at confirmation (it feels very *Earthsea* and Ursula Le Guin). That said, if I had taken a new name at fifteen, you would now be calling me Raphael – after the Teenage Mutant Ninja Turtle, of course. (JW)

Servers or choristers

One means of harnessing the skills and gifts of children and young people in a church service is to give them key roles that they might wish to perform. In an Anglican church where the service leaders have robes, it is hardly surprising that identifying significant children's roles with robes meets with some interest. At the first church where I was vicar, the practice was for children to be "servers", a role in which they wore a white cassock. Servers were required to be acolytes and to carry the candles necessary for the public reading of the Gospel, or to be the crucifer and carry the cross at the front of the procession. Other children were welcomed into the choir, where similarly they were robed as choristers.

All these roles became desirable to the young people of the church and in some cases were competed for. While I am aware that many churches do not process or have choirs, I will always recall the huge value that such roles gave to children wanting to be part of the service. I have rarely seen servers or choristers misusing their role and have often seen even quite small children adding huge dignity to their office.

> None of us can sing, but my brothers and I all served at the altar in my dad's church in Radford, Nottingham. This was largely an excuse for us to look angelic while trying to set each other's hair on fire as acolytes. Seriously, though, it felt good to be involved and a part of the ritual. (JW)

Youth group services

Much has been written about the various merits of organizing Sunday schools (or children's church) or youth groups, but key to this literature is the general intent to include children and young people into the current worshipping life of the church. As Bob Jackson has demonstrated in his research on church growth (2002, 2005, and 2006), churches that invest in children's ministry are more likely to grow.

In recent years, the practice of segregating children into age-related groups has begun to be critiqued in that, although it accommodates the needs of children, it is hugely resource intensive and moreover does not always succeed in integrating them into the main congregation.

What does seem to have high impact in terms of integration is the joyful and risky experience of handing the entire church service over to the young people themselves, so that they can lead the liturgy, read the lessons, lead the worship and the intercessions, and even preach or lead the main act of reflection. Such a service will allow the young people to step up as leaders and it will moreover cause the main congregation to become engaged with the ideas and culture of younger people. Of course, this calls for skilled youth leadership in mentoring the young people to do this. In churches that I have led, this habit has not been without objection from some of the congregation, but it has definitely been worthwhile in terms of getting the young people to feel they have a distinctive contribution and in adding a focus to the youth ministry. It is probably the single most influential means of encouraging young people to feel that they have a role to play in the church of today. From a parent's point of view, such a practice in the church generates vast amounts of reflection and discussion.

Research from the Church of England entitled "Rooted in the Church"

In November 2016, the Church of England's Education Office commissioned an investigation to explore the relationship between the church and its young people in order to better understand what helps them stay rooted. This report, called "Rooted in the Church", was building on an earlier document called "From Anecdote to Evidence" (2014), which noted that growing secularization is causing each generation to be "less religious than the one before". It was keen to discover why some people go against this trend by being "rooted in the church". It also draws on the Church Growth Research Programme's claim that:

> there is no single recipe for growth... Growth depends
> on the context, and what works in one place may
> not work in another. There are no strong connections
> between growth and worship style, theological
> tradition, and so on. Growth is a product of good
> leadership (lay and ordained) working with a willing
> set of churchgoers in a favourable environment.

It notes that the issue of declining youth attendance and affiliation is not confined to churches. Evidence shows that other types of membership clubs, sports organizations, and voluntary associations also struggle to retain young people beyond the age of 16 – a trend that is linked to a drop in "social connectedness".

While the church is not just a membership group and is also a body of fellowship and faith, the report accepts that the engagement of young people with the church has a lot to do with the so-called secularization thesis.

The key findings of "Rooted in the Church" were as follows:

- Overall, the majority of young people said that, in their opinion, the most important attribute of a church should be that it is "friendly" and "non-judgmental". In other words, inclusion is an important issue even after periods of absence from church.

- Young people considered that inclusion within "the whole church family" should be reflected in the style of worship: while they value age-specific leadership and activities, they do not want to always be artificially separated from the main church.
- Young people want to be treated as equal members of the church. They want to have meaningful roles that include leadership and serving opportunities, and intergenerational ministry. They would also like to have a greater "voice and vote" on decision-making bodies such as PCCs and synods.
- Intergenerational relationships in the church are important, highlighting the need for "bridge people" who work through small groups to include young people within the wider church community. This model contrasts with one that separates young people and youth leaders from the wider church. Youth workers are the ideal "bridge people", yet their work is often not sufficiently resourced or supported.
- Young people's engagement with faith is not a binary question of attendance – being "in" church or "out" of it. There are types and stages of disengagement that have been labelled by experts as:

  - nomads;
  - exiles;
  - prodigals;
  - switchers;
  - reverters; and
  - unbelievers.

- The issue of youth attendance and affiliation is not confined to churches alone. Similar patterns of disengagement can be found in declining levels of participation in other membership groups, including sports and voluntary clubs.
- Young adults who state that Christianity is important in their daily lives demonstrate higher levels of participation in other types of voluntary clubs and membership groups than those who do not state that Christianity is important in their daily lives.

Listening to the insights of children

Much can be said about how children might be better valued in the home or in the church, but key to it all will be the extent to which their insights are gleaned and reflected upon. Back in 2010 I concluded an article entitled "The Bible in the Family Context" (2010b), summing up a vision for what might happen when children's insights are listened to carefully. As I consider how church might be included as part of the kingdom dream, my reflections remain consistent.

This project has successfully managed to access data from an intimate and rarely seen source, namely the family home. From this data it is possible to offer guidelines of best practice for parents, teachers and ministers using Bible stories.

However, secondary research insight discovered that parental interpretation often offers an assumed literalism that is likely to impede future development in children's understanding of story. If children's insights are to be heard as they encounter the Bible, they must be allowed to engage with the text. This is done when the storyteller stands further back from the text and allows the child to engage with it imaginatively. The Bible is often told via the familial route of a parent or the authoritative route of the church minister. The parent (or the minister) can allow the child to wrestle with the text to identify meaning for themselves to critique what is being said. Possibly the new storytellers will offer a Pullman-like daringness to decode the text or a Lewis-like imagination to re-interpret it. When this is done, our task will be to interpret the child's voice from the different filters that have been set in place. Maybe a way to develop the research stories is to remove the genre classifications from the stories and ask children to comment on them without any steer at all as to how others might interpret them. This would further allow for the original vision of the child to be heard as they encounter Scripture.

In the same way, my vision is that the church will allow children's voices to be heard to inform it in how to operate so that the children are at home at church and are genuinely included.

A new dream of what church might be

I am aware that this chapter on making churchgoing a habit sits uneasily with me. Why is this, when my life is so dominated by church? I remain active in regular ministry every weekend, and during the week my wonderful job is to train church ministers. My wife is a bishop and she adds a wider perspective on the national church. Yet still I am concerned that church can take the place of God. Deep down I am aware that religion can screen spirituality. In trying to achieve orthodox faith, the church so easily becomes a legal institution or an oppressor of the marginalized.

So I dare to dream of a different church from the one I know so well. I dream of a church that is open to the Spirit and true to the historic revelation of Jesus in the Bible. That church will enjoy diversity and not be afraid of holding a range of divergent views within the congregation.

How will church become like this? It will be divergent because it makes space to listen, to love, and to respect. It will allow the Christians who are part of it to express their views from their different cultures, age perspectives, and experiences of life. I dream of a church where a child offers wise insight that is only apparent to a young mind. I imagine a church where the perspective of the person with a learning difficulty is heard alongside the perspectives of those without any learning difficulties. I long for a church that makes space for the cultural and theological contributions of Africa or Asia or messianic Judaism.

The only way that such diversity will ever find expression is if people meet regularly and eat together. Therefore my dream of church is more akin to an extended family, where people meet in small units in the home and in larger gatherings as church and maybe in huge gatherings for celebration. This church may well offer the daily routine of "new monasticism", in which members have the opportunity for daily and evening prayer and for eating together on some days, but it will also be outward looking. I prefer the notion of the friar to the monk, because I picture the friar to have a remit for going out and about on a mission rather than for retreating to the cell. So I'd call this "new Franciscanism", a form of regular meeting but with the mission of making Jesus known and loved in all the world. If church were like this, I'd be deeply happy. So let me be a part of building this vision of the kingdom and I believe it will take off.

I half suspect that my sons, whom I have raised in the faith, will one day become ministers in the church of the future, but I believe that if they do so they will see this vision of church better than I do. If they become ordained or accredited ministers, or if they remain as active lay members, my prayer is that they will be building a revolutionary kingdom church, not maintaining the institutional church.

(B) When We Despised the Church (Failing to accept God's body)

I plead with Euodia and I plead with Syntyche to be of the same mind in the Lord.

(Philippians 4:2)

In most gatherings of churchgoing Christian parents with grown-up children, it does not take long to discover that high on their list of conversation topics is likely to be whether their children still attend church. And this topic is not peculiar to Christian parents. From wider engagement with Muslims and through reading

Islamic research literature, I hear a similar interest focused on whether the next generation will continue to attend the mosque.

Among those Christians who discuss their children's churchgoing habits, considerable guilt seems to be felt by those whose children no longer express interest in church. They feel that they have failed. They rarely suggest that this is connected to secularization, but they often hint that it is likely to be their fault as parents.

Why is this? In nearly every situation it is not that the parents have been other than faithful to God, highly observant in engaging with church, and normally creative in their attempts to nurture their children in the faith. Surely their perceived guilt lies in the fact that whether their children still believe is of importance to them; it matters to them as parents whether or not their children hold similar values, but it is something over which they have no control. Therefore, when they realize that their children no longer prioritize church, they believe they have failed.

To those parents I want to say three things:

- Faith is a gift of God – not a gift that we as parents can dispense to our children. Our job is to pass on the story and make it available to the next generation.
- We as parents need to trust God for our children, and in giving our children freedom to choose, we do what God has done to us in giving us freedom.
- Our children have new insights from their own generation and they might be more able to see some of the residual viruses and sins of the previous generation, including our religion, and as such we need to trust the judgment of their adult choices.

Having said this, I am aware that there have been some ways in which my own parenting style has not always allowed my own children to engage with church. In fact, there have been times when my very love of the church must have been deeply off-putting. Chief among these has been the ways in which I have allowed my negative feelings about church to be expressed to them. I have not hidden from my sons that at times I have despised the institution known as church.

I believe I have done this in two ways: first, by talking the church down (through gossip and rejection) and, second, by calling certain Christians "fundamentalists" or "liberals".

Talking the church down (through gossip and rejection)

It is strange that we tend to be hardest on those we love best and most critical of those who are closest to us. Possibly it is because the church is of such importance to us that we can be most critical of it and similarly why we are hurt when the public representation of church is derided. Maybe this is why we feel most damaged when the church's reputation is in tatters. Personally, it is when I have invested my deepest hopes in projects connected to the church, and when the church has not cared for those projects to the extent that I have, that I have become most critical of the church.

It is that criticism of church that I fear I sometimes allowed to be heard within the family home and I fear will have jaundiced the boys while they were growing up. For me it was impossible to keep the private and the professional worlds separate, as we lived in the vicarage, so there were times when the toxicity of church politics seeped into the family home.

I can recall at one time being plagued by daily letters from a member of the church, a person who (I was subsequently to discover) had psychological problems and was out of work. She had the time to write reams every day, followed up by visits to the vicarage and frequent phone calls. I felt trapped, and vented my feelings on more than one occasion. Such criticism was hardly likely to have been of value to the growing children.

I disagree. Hearing your parents' frustration reminds you that they are human and feel things like you do. But then I have grown up to be a misanthrope and am likely to find reasons to justify my own poor behaviour. (JW)

On another occasion, as Vice-Chair for the Board of Education, I became the project officer for the development of a new school in the diocese. To me this was an exciting project for mission among young people – something that required resources, energy, and vision – but it failed to attract the bishop's imagination and he considered it to be a high-risk venture. As a result I was left representing the diocese in high-level talks with the local authority without any sense of the institution's backing. It was a project that needed fast action, and I found myself carving out policies that I could not guarantee would be honoured. On that occasion, within the family home I became highly critical of the diocesan structures and the bishop in particular. In the event, the school became a huge success and when the risk had cleared it was finally given episcopal blessing. Again my cynicism was articulated within earshot of the boys. Such venting might have been of some value to myself as a parent under pressure, but it was hardly likely to have been a means of edifying young minds.

Looking at the scriptural records, this sin of low-level whingeing was what caused Moses to be criticized by Yahweh. Similarly, it was the moaning of the children of Israel in the desert of Sinai that caused Yahweh to punish them. In other words, it was careless talk that was to cause the deeper-seated culture of criticism that resulted in the Israelites being rebuked. It was not a sin without consequences.

Calling certain Christians "fundamentalists" or "liberals"

One of the most helpful and memorable titles of any book on my bookshelves is *Never Call Them Jerks* by A. P. Boers. In a few pages it summarizes that the demonization of the other is never helpful in any encounter, as all people are made in God's image, even if they are not acting in a way that shows this.

Within the church we need to be constantly reminded that some of the last words from the historic Jesus were recorded in a lengthy prayer that his disciples would be as one (John 17:21). This prayer speaks with deep insight into the human condition, in that for many of us our default position is to divide in order to conquer rather than to unite and love. Church history is littered with division.

In our current twenty-first-century church we might have learned to be more respectful across the ancient denominational rifts. It is now generally accepted that different denominations have different strengths and show something of the diversity and richness of Christian mission. Within the different church denominations there is increasing variety, allowing low church and high church perspectives to be found within one denomination and often within one cluster of churches in a given area. However, when it comes to issues of conflict, we often resort to dubbing the other as either "too fundamentalist" or "too liberal".

The "fundamentalist" tag is often offered to perspectives that we find too conservative. Maybe they are viewpoints that appear too legalistic or too literal to the interpretation of Scripture held by us. Alternatively, the "liberal" tag is offered to perspectives that are wider than our own; those viewpoints that are looser with Scripture or appear to be less theologically defined.

As a parent of young children growing up within the Christian faith, I fear that I did call some people "jerks" as well as "liberals" or "fundamentalists", depending on the issue or indeed the time of day. I wonder how young minds survived such dismissive thinking from a parent who also affirmed a gospel of grace and love.

Aware of this, as a parent I wrote a poem entitled "Modern Warfare", which endeavoured to portray the fight going on between the younger generation and the older. I depicted the younger generation kindly as fighting under the banner of Grace and riding white steeds, whereas the older generation were fighting under the banner of Truth and riding dark horses.

Modern Warfare

The armies stood on two opposing hills,
Each resplendent in their bright array,
Each claiming rights to land held by the other,
And seeking combat for the outcome.

Pitched towards the rising sun stood "Grace",
A force that won where others lost,
Her banners fluttered words accepting,
Her champions were young and hopeful.

But "Truth" was camped on moral's high ground,
Supremely sure her cause was just.
Her standards stood for righteousness,
Her warriors were old but strong.

There came a horseman from the west camp,
His charger white, his banner peaceful.
His war cry rang out loud and clear,
"Take me as I am!"

In turn there issued from the East
A sturdy warhorse, black and steely,
Whose rider ordered to the four winds,
"Take the path of Truth!"

The clash rang out within the valley,
And mighty was the fight.
Love's helm was crushed, Truth's belt was split
And blood flowed on the ground.

The battle waged both day and night,
The champions changed to fight all week.
New issues came, debates unearthed,
The war went on all year.

For centuries the battle raged,
Defectors went from West to East,
With Western warriors breeding well
And Eastern champions dying full of years.

And still the fight goes on somewhere,
In lands afar and by my hearth.
Young blood baying for acceptance,
Tradition blocking with her standards.
Old blood thundering down with Truth,
New ways dancing past with Grace.

Final thoughts

I'll keep it short and sweet. My experience of being parented and my experience of coming to faith have been the same thing.

It has been a shared family adventure in which I was allowed a real and respected opinion about what I thought of God, church, and my place in the universe. Both my dad and mum and my brothers seemed to expect actual insight from some of what I said.

While working as an outdoor instructor I have had many interesting talks with people aged around twelve. Often I have become aware that this may be the first time an adult has had a real one-to-one conversation with them! Not just a teacher talking to them and thirty others, or a parent asking them what they've done at school or when they're going to tidy their bedrooms, but a real conversation in which their ideas are genuinely insightful to the adult.

And that's just it. If you expect actual conversation and ask genuinely interesting questions of a child then you will receive actual conversation and genuinely interesting answers!

If you want a child to engage with God and take seriously what you say, then all you have to do is take their answers seriously, and maybe even expect to learn something of God from them. (NW)

For discussion

- Do you agree with the sentence, "When churches treat young people as customers, they feel that they can shop elsewhere, but when they are treated as family, they are more likely to join in with proceedings"?
- In church, various aspects of best practice are offered to enable young people to feel included. Are there any you would add (or omit)?
- Do you agree that ultimately parents need to trust their children to make up their own minds about faith, God, and church?
- Can you relate to the author's lament at being such a harsh critic of church? Do you think that it is this sin that puts off the next generation?
- Discuss the last stanza of the poem. How do you perceive the warfare near you?

And still the fight goes on somewhere,
In lands afar and by my hearth.
Young blood baying for acceptance,

Tradition blocking with her standards.
Old blood thundering down with Truth,
New ways dancing past with Grace.

Conclusion

So there you have it: my five best habits and my five worst vices as a parent, distilled and put into print. Having written them I feel both pleased and a little coy. Pleased because these reflections are what I deeply believe and they have taken me a while to distil, but coy because they are now open to critique. Normally when I write, I enjoy being critiqued and even deliberately create a debate, but that is when I am in my comfort zone of the academy. In that context I can hold my ideas at arm's length. By contrast, not only is this book deeply personal, it is also obviously incomplete, because as a parent I too am a work in progress. What I have written is now open to you the readers to consider in your own parenting lives, and I'm sure you will improve on my parenting.

I think that my particular vulnerability is that I have opened up the private world of my home – a place so rarely laid bare to the outside world. But I'm not too embarrassed, because my three sons have all added their comments to my writings. I know I have said nothing that I haven't discussed with them, but as for my wife, the lovely Bishop of Taunton, that's another story. That is why she has written the foreword.

Of all that has been written, my greatest surprise and delight has been to note that my boys have disagreed with my categorization of good and bad habits. Where I thought I had succeeded as a parent, they were less sure. When I thought I had failed, they suggested that I might have succeeded. The evidence for this was stated way back at the beginning of the book when Ben wrote, "These 'cock-ups' of parenting are clearly at least as important as the good habits. I have enjoyed reading these the most." In a similar vein, Nathanael wrote, "While Dad has clearly separated each chapter into 'When it worked' and 'When it did not work', this logical separating of good from bad is not how it works in the real world."

These comments delight me because the subject material of parenting is complex, and the criteria for its success are not easily discernible. However, the people most qualified to comment on parenting are those who have experienced it. So I'll gladly listen to those comments from my sons.

In the end, I believe that our parenting is done before God and it is God alone who judges. In fact, Scripture teaches us that it is God alone who grants the gift of faith, so how not to totally put your children off God can be said to be entirely God's business. But that is a cop-out. Somehow we all know that we as parents do play a part. I guess parenting must be a joint effort in which we partner with God.

To finish, I'll let Nathanael have the last word. Talking about the end result of parenting, he says, "Things have a habit of growing together and it's not until much later that you can determine whether the fruit is sweet or bitter. This to me draws very strong parallels of Jesus' parable of the wheat and the chaff." So that is how it will be. We offer our best parenting in the power of the Spirit. Put another way, we act with the wisdom that God offers and we leave the rest to him. With apologies to St Paul (whom I am shamelessly plagiarizing from 1 Corinthians 3:5–11), I believe that, had he written about parenting, he might have said:

What is this parent or that parent? They are only servants of God, through whom you came into being – as the Lord gave each a task. One parent planted the seed, another nurtured it, but God made the child grow up. So neither the one who plants nor the one who nurtures is to be praised or condemned. It is actually God who enables the child to develop. The one who plants and the one who nurtures have one purpose in parenting, and they will each be rewarded according to their own labour. For we are co-workers in God's service. As parents, you are God's field, God's building. By the grace God has given me, I laid a foundation as a parent, and someone else is building on it. But each one should build with care. For no one can lay any foundation other than the one already laid, which is Jesus Christ.

Further Reading

Berryman, J. (1995) *Godly Play*, Minneapolis, MN: Augsburg.

Berryman, J. (2009) *Children and the Theologians: Clearing the Way for Grace*, New York: Morehouse Publishing.

Bettelheim, B. (1976) *The Uses of Enchantment: The Meaning and Importance of Fairytales*, London: Penguin.

Boers, A. P. (1999) *Never Call Them Jerks*, Louisville: The Alban Institute

Bridger, F. (2001) *A Charmed Life: The Spirituality of Potterworld*, London: Darton, Longman and Todd.

Church of England (2014) "From Anecdote to Evidence", London: Church House Publishing.

Church of England Education Office (2016) "Rooted in the Church", London: Church House Publishing.

Cox, R. (2000) *Using the Bible with Children*, Grove Booklet B15, Cambridge: Grove Books.

Cox, R. (2001) "Using the Bible with Children", *Journal of Education and Christian Belief*, 5(1), I I 1–118.

Dawkins, R. (2007) *The God Delusion*, London: Black Swan.

Erikson, E. (1950) *Childhood and Society*, New York: Norton.

Fowler, J. (1981) *Stages of Faith*, San Francisco: Harper & Row.

Fowler, J. (1986) "Stages of Faith" in Joann Wolski Conn (ed.) *Women's Spirituality: Resources for Christian Development*, Paulist, pp. 226–32.

Fowler, J. (2004) "Faith Development at 30: Naming the Challenges of Faith in a New Millennium", *Religious Education*, Vol. 99, No. 4, pp. 405–21.

Goebbel, R. & G. Goebbel (1986) *The Bible: a Child's Playground*, London: SCM Press.

Goldman, R. (1964) *Religious Thinking from Childhood to Adolescence*, London: Routledge & Kegan Paul.

Goldman, R. (1965) *Readiness for Religion*, London: Routledge & Kegan Paul.

Gosse, E. (1907) *Father and Son: A Study of Two Temperaments*, London: Penguin (1989)

Graystone, P. (1989) *Help! There's a Child in My Church*, Milton Keynes: Scripture Union

Hammarskjöld, Dag (2006) *Markings*, New York: Vintage Books.

Jackson, B. (2002) *Hope for the Church: Contemporary Strategies for Growth*, London: Church House Publishing.

Jackson, B. (2005) *The Road to Growth: Towards a Thriving Church*, London: Church House Publishing.

Jackson, B. (2006) *Going for Growth: What Works at Local Church Level*, London: Church House Publishing.

Jennings, T. W. (2006) *Reading Derrida/Thinking Paul*, Stanford, CA: Stanford University Press.

Kingsolver, B. (1998) *The Poisonwood Bible*, New York: Harper.

Marshall, I. H. (1992) "Atonement in the New Testament", *Anchor Bible Dictionary*, New York: Doubleday

Parsons, R. (2009) *The Sixty Minute Father*, London: Hodder & Stoughton.

Piaget, J. (1928) *The Child's Conception of the World*, London: Kegan Paul.

Pike, M. (2003) "Belief as an Obstacle to Reading: The Case of the Bible?", *Journal of Beliefs and Values*, 24(2), pp. 55–63.

Polyani, M. (1966) *The Tacit Dimension*, Chicago: University of Chicago Press.

Robinson, E. (1977) *The Original Vision: A Study of the Religious Experience of Childhood*, Oxford: Religious Experience Research Centre.

Smith, J. K. A. (2000) *The Fall of Interpretation: Philosophical Foundations for a Creational Hermeneutic*, Downers Grove, IL: IVP.

Vygotsky, L. S. (1962) *Thought and Language*, Cambridge, MA: MIT Press.

Wither, M. (2010) *Mission-Shaped Children: Moving Towards a Child-Centred Church*, London: Church House Publishing

Worsley, H. J. (2004) "Popularised Atonement Theory Reflected in Children's Literature", *The Expository Times*, Vol. 115, No. 5, February, pp. 149–56.

Worsley, H. J. (2009) *A Child Sees God*, London: Jessica Kingsley.

Worsley, H. J. (2010a) "Children's Literature as Implicit Religion: The Concept of Grace Unpacked", *Journal of Implicit Religion*, Vol .13, No. 1, April.

Worsley, H. J. (2010b) "The Bible in the Family Context", *International Journal of Children's Spirituality*, Vol. 15, No. 2, May, pp. 115–27.